THE LEAST OF THESE

A REMARKABLE TRUE STORY OF GOD'S MERCY, GRACE AND AWESOME POWER TO SAVE

THE LEAST OF THESE

A REMARKABLE TRUE STORY OF GOD'S MERCY, GRACE AND AWESOME POWER TO SAVE

DANIEL MARK LUKE

Christmas Carol Books

Denver • Salt Lake City • Los Angeles

©2016 Daniel Mark Luke

All rights reserved. No part of this book may be reproduced in any form or by any means without permission in writing from the publisher, Christmas Carol Books. The experiences and views herein expressed are the sole responsibility of the author.

Library of Congress Cataloging in Publication Data
Luke, Daniel Mark, 1963
The Least of These / Daniel M. Luke

A remarkable true story of God's mercy, grace and awesome power to save.

ISBN 978-1-944782-66-5 (hardbound)
ISBN 978-944784-95-9 (softcover)
also available as an e-Book on Amazon Kindle

Layout and book design by Patrick K. Hill
Hill Studio & Design, Kaysville, Utah

Printed in the United States of America
Carr Printing Co., Bountiful, Utah

Thanks, Mom and Dad, for all the love, support and the encouragement to try

Christmas Carol Books
PO Box 42
Farmington, Utah 84025

—

First printing Summer 2016

To Heavenly Father ~
Who made it all happen, that all may believe.

and to Tauna ~
My personal lifeguard who can't swim, along with the
others who were with me that day.

*"...Go home to thy friends,
and tell them how great things the Lord
hath done for thee, and hath
had compassion on thee."*

—

Mark 5:19

TABLE OF CONTENTS

PART I
Angel's Story 15

PART II
Angels Unaware 55

PART III
Angels Among Us 95

Acknowledgements 111

INTRODUCTION

Our fear and fascination of sharks is universal.

We're mesmerized by them at public aquariums, and we cannot take our eyes off of them.

Every summer, the news brings us a seemingly increasing number of encounters with the ocean's apex predators, sometimes even with shocking video. It's reported that worldwide there are between ten and thirty fatalities each year.

A dear friend of mine was once an eyewitness to a deadly attack, and I too — were it not for Heavenly Father's grace — would have been a victim of the same fate.

But I'm getting ahead of the story...

Martin Luther

King, Jr. Day

We celebrate each January 19th, because of what happened here on August 28, 1963.

14

PART I
Angel's Story

"...there shall none come into this land save they shall be brought by the hand of the Lord."
—
2 Nephi 1:6

I am neither a scholar, an academic, or a theologian, but I *do* know that I wouldn't be able to tell this story without the help of an angel. It's only with thanks to a good man from Cuba, by the name of Angel Avila Ochoa that I do so. Sadly, the last time I saw him alive was on Wednesday, August 28, 2013.

It was the 50th anniversary of Dr. Martin Luther King's famous "I Have a Dream" speech, and also my fiftieth birthday. Yep, the speech in our nation's capital which galvanized the Civil Rights Movement was on the very day that my dear mother gave birth to me three thousand miles away on the west coast.

Turning the big five-o felt pretty cool, knowing that the entire nation was looking back a half-century along with me that day. As in years past, there was the famous black and white TV footage from 1963 of the Mall in Washington, D.C., with thousands of marchers gathered all around the reflecting pool. In the background stands the Washington Monument at the opposite end of the mall, facing Dr. King as he gives one of the greatest speeches in our nation's history. As I was getting dressed for work, the morning news shows were full of purpose and in a celebratory mood, with smiles all around as they reflected on the big day.

Every August since I can remember, the media has

marked the occasion by broadcasting the images of the famous speech on the network news. This year when the day arrived, there was an extra special feeling to it all for me, as it isn't everyday that you and the whole nation get to celebrate a Golden Anniversary together.

I arrived at work, and we began the day on the workroom floor, sorting the mail for our routes. While we do this, things are generally low key and pretty quiet. My buddy Ryan, a thirty year man at the Post Office, nodded and said, "Hey, Daniel-san!" in his best *Karate Kid* imitation. He then mentioned something about yesterday's sports news like he always does.

With his personality and salt and pepper mustache, Ryan has a passing resemblance to the mailman on the old *Cheers* television show from the '90s. The local high school kids gave him the nickname "Cliffie" back then, which he didn't like at first, but now he smiles and wears it as a badge of honor. Ryan is also the only guy I've ever known to get 100 percent on the entrance exam the Postal Service administers to new applicants. He's a man of high integrity, and I hope to be able to pull off a miracle someday, and retire with him still at my side.

We noted the anniversary of Dr. King's speech, and Ryan said he couldn't believe that fifty years had already passed, as he remembers watching it on TV as a little boy. He's an older gentleman with a great sense of humor, and he chuckled a bit when I told him that was my big day too. The conversation died down, and we settled into our work.

Then I got the news about Angel's cancer.

We'd been at it for about half an hour, when the letter carrier who delivers to my friend's house turned from across the room and said, "Dan, Angel has cancer." I was stunned. You're never prepared to hear that kind of thing. "What? When did that happen?" It was all I could say. "I don't know," was the reply. "They say he has only two months to live though."

Cancer is never welcome news — but to learn that his initial diagnosis was terminal, and that he only had weeks to live made it extra shocking and hard to believe.

I stammered. "Where is he — at his house?" "No," was the reply. "He's at a facility in Ogden, and probably won't be coming home." That put a stop to any thoughts I had that morning about my birthday, Dr. King — everything. It was all I could think about, and yet I still had to prepare my route for a whole day of deliveries. It was suddenly hard to concentrate, but I pushed through. It was difficult, but I knew that nothing can stop the U.S. Mail.

At the end of the day I went home and picked up my wife, and without changing out of my uniform, we drove directly to the care center to see Angel. I usually can't wait to get home and get myself cleaned up and changed into fresh clothes. I especially would have wanted to make myself presentable for an occasion like this, but I felt a sense of urgency, and so within thirty minutes of clocking off at work, we arrived at his room.

He was there all by himself, with only his big TV and a photo of his mother leaning against it. Sitting upright in a chair, he was experiencing some pain, but nevertheless was glad to see us. We visited with him for only a few minutes, telling him that we had just heard the news, and had come right over. Comforting him as best we could, we gave him our love, and told him how much he has meant to our family. We wished the boys could have been there as well. A tearful blessing was pronounced at the close of our short visit, which brought a measure of peace in a difficult time. We parted with hugs, and promised him we'd be back in a few days.

Saturday morning the 31st of August, we returned with a small Cuban flag that had been in his living room in Kaysville, and a compact disc of music from his beloved island. I wanted to bring him whatever we could to make his last days as comfortable as possible. We went into his room, and were stunned to see it empty. They gave him two months to live, but he was gone in three days.

I was grateful that his suffering was brief, and also thankful we got to see him one last time. President Monson is right about responding promptly when inspired to do so.

The following Monday, after delivering to the bank on Main street, I glanced up to where Angel had lived. His was the first home on the right, at 24 East Crestwood. It was a small white house, maybe 30 feet by 30 feet, with two big columns on the front porch. There was enough space for a couple of chairs where he'd sit and wave at me as I drove by his house and honked.

I had just visited him a few weeks before and he seemed fine, with no health problems. He was very content and happy, seemingly on top of the world. Angel was retired and full of life, and there was no indication that he was enjoying his last summer.

Thinking back a few weeks, President Monson was right — again. Two months earlier in mid-June, I had an impression that I should go see my old friend, as it had been quite awhile since I had spent some time with him. We had been amigos since the late 1990s, when I met Angel at his first job in town.

He took care of the grounds and building at the newly opened McDonald's franchise. It was connected to a Chevron station on 200 North, just off the freeway exit to our small city of Kaysville, north of Salt Lake City.

Kaysville was Davis County's first incorporated city in 1868. Though originally a farming community, it has been quite progressive and industrious among all of Utah's cities. In 1903, the first telephone exchange was created in Kaysville, serving the entire county. Long ago their engineers built the city-owned power plant, providing inexpensive electricity to its citizens. Lucky us!

The heart and soul of Kaysville is the 100 year old Davis High School, with its tradition of academic and athletic excellence. There's also a popular dollar theater on Main Street, and the historic LDS Kaysville Tabernacle is beautiful inside and out. Its stained glass windows remind me of those at the Assembly Hall on Temple Square, and it was a privilege to worship there when we first moved to Kaysville in 1992. Dedicated in 1914 with its distinctive yellow clay bricks, it stands as a monument to the pioneers and their sons who built it.

Besides its rich LDS history, Kaysville is also home to one of the first Presbyterian churches in Utah. Built in 1888, it was designed by the same local architect who worked on the Tabernacle. It's a charming little chapel in the center of town, and is currently used by the Pentecostals of Utah. Also in town, African Americans from all over the Salt Lake Valley attend the True Vine Baptist Church; and the Kaysville Bible Church is just down the street from our home on Flint Street.

My hometown is a bit like Mayberry, and yet big and diverse enough to be welcoming to all. I truly believe the good Reverend Dr. King would feel comfortable preaching from the pulpit of any of the churches in our city.

Among the LDS faithful, Kaysville is perhaps best known for being the place where John Taylor, the third President of the Church resided until his death in 1887.

Among Kaysville's noteworthy citizens from the past, are two who made a world-wide impact and yet are perhaps not known by today's generation. They are Dr. Sumner Gleason and Floyd Gottfredson. In 1915, Dr. Gleason was a nationally known horticulturist, who developed the famous Gleason Elberta peach. This tree is sold at nurseries nationwide each spring, and its fruit is loved by millions.

Floyd Gottfredson was a young boy in Kaysville in the early 1920s, who was left with a disabled arm, following a hunting accident. This limited his participation in typical children's activities of the day, so he took correspondence courses in art. He developed his artistic abilities, and in 1929, he moved to California and began working for Walt Disney. After only a few weeks as his employee, he was given the job of drawing the world-wide Mickey Mouse comic strip. For nearly the next fifty years, millions who saw Disney's most famous character in the funnies, were enjoying the creative work of Kaysville's Floyd Gottfredson.

In the late 1990s, when I met Angel, we had about 16,000 residents in our little community, but there was much growth projected, especially on the west side of the I-15 freeway. There, the farm land was quickly being divided up for future development, which would eventually double our city's size and population. That's where we are today.

The new McDonald's and service station built at that time made it feel like we were finally 'on the map' so to speak, as a growing city — and Angel was the one hired to be the care-taker of this important addition to our hometown.

He was there each morning before the crack of dawn with a hose in his hand, washing down the parking lot. Dressed in his McDonald's golf-shirt and ball hat, he took care of business every day, with no small measure of pride in how he did his job. Always, he had a great big smile on his face as he worked. It was part of his uniform. He was so cool.

He was in his late forties back in 1997, but looked young-er. The years had been good to him, and I suspect that it was due in part to his positive attitude. He stood about 5'- 8" tall, and weighed about 180 pounds. He was trim, and darker in complexion, as are many from the Caribbean — who are descendants from a mix of the native Indian tribes along with the great numbers of Africans who were brought there in the 18th century.

A lesser known fact is that nearly half of all the slaves brought to the New World ended up on the isles of the Greater Antilles — the islands of: Hispañola, (present-day countries of the Dominican Republic and Haiti), Cuba and

Puerto Rico, and what became the U.S. and British Virgin Islands. Others were brought, or migrated to the Lesser Antilles — the small chain of islands that curve in an arc from Puerto Rico south.

They were the islands where I was called to serve as a missionary in 1983, in the San Juan Puerto Rico Mission. These smaller islands were composed of, but not limited to: St. Martin, St. Kitts, Aruba, Tortuga, Dominica, Guadalupe, St. Lucia, Barbados, and Trinidad and Tobago.

I worked among the islanders of the Caribbean, as well as with the Latinos on the Mexican border, and found their culture to be rich, festive, and exciting. These people are passionate about life, and are humble and grateful for every opportunity that comes their way.

Cuba and Puerto Rico are two of the larger neighboring islands in the Caribbean, and I therefore felt a special kinship with Angel from the beginning. The people on both islands speak the Spanish language quite fast, and with a similar accent. The flags of the two nations are nearly identical as well.

Puerto Rico is a free associated-state of the United States, and its flag has elements of the American flag. There are horizontal red and white stripes, and a triangular blue field on the left, with one large white star in it. The Cuban flag is just the opposite, with blue and white stripes, and a field of red with one white star.

Angel was handsome — with a quick smile and large expressive eyes, and short dark hair. He had an athletic build, and looked quite a bit like the Dominican baseball hero Sammy Sosa, who at that time was belting home runs for the Chicago Cubs. I'd tell him, "Angel, you look like Sammy, only shorter!" which made him smile, and we would both laugh. "Béisbol" is his nation's favorite sport, so he'd smile all the broader — being compared to such a Latin star.

In his native Cuba, the government just recently relaxed a five decade ban on professional ball players leaving the island to play elsewhere. Since September of 2013, a full quarter of the players on their star-studded World's Baseball Classic team have left the island in search of major league deals. Who can blame them? The contracts for six of the top earning Cuban-born major leaguers today add up to nearly $300 million. That's a good chunk of Cuba's 1.6 billion dollar yearly gross national product. Not bad for only six of their citizens in the free market. Let's hear an "Amen" for Free Enterprise!

Many other ball players have been allowed to go to Japan or Mexico to play in their respective leagues, as long as a large chunk of their income goes back to the Communist State — *and* they agree to return to the island to play in the Cuban League each September. How magnanimous of their government. That's how much Angel and all Cubans love their baseball.

Angel was an easy-going guy, with a voice similar to that of actor Peter Falk, in his role as the TV detective *Columbo*, only in Spanish. He had a limited knowledge of the English language, but was friendly and tried his best with everyone he met. Sometimes all he'd need was his warm smile to make friends, so he made out alright. I felt very lucky to be one of them.

He started his day at 4:30 am, by doing 200 push-ups, then getting cleaned up and walking the two blocks from the motel where he lived at the time, to his job at McDonald's. There, he turned on the ovens for his co-workers to cook and prepare the breakfast burritos and other items for the morning customers who would come in over the next few hours.

Then he ate his favorite breakfast, which was an order of two steak and egg bagels with an orange juice. "*Mucha proteina!*" he'd say as he flexed both of his bicep muscles a la Schwarzenegger. He'd tell me it fueled his exercise routine. To hear it from a rock solid guy who does 200 early morning pushups ...that the buttered and toasted bagels with juicy steaks on them — are actually GOOD FOR YOU...that sounded good to me! — I mean, he had abs and shoulders like a 28 year-old well-conditioned athlete...and for him to look that solid at his age while eating two greasy steaks on toasted bagels every morning — well suffice it to say, I was pretty impressed! So much for today's so-called conventional wisdom!

It was just the beginning of many surprising and very interesting things I was to learn about my new Cuban friend, which I would like to share with you.

He was exacting and tried very hard to do his best. He felt lucky to have a job, and was a hard worker, as are so many of the people who make it to the United States from Latin America. Many times they are among the earliest to rise, doing jobs that many consider menial here in the states — but that are as necessary and important as any other blue or white collar job. It's vitally important to them and their families, as it is to me and mine. I actually share something in common with them, as we've had a family-owned commercial cleaning business since the 1980s. Lots of people go to the gym to work out. We just go to work, and believe me, it's a workout!

When I first met Angel, I was cleaning offices in the evenings with my wife and three young boys, Christopher, Michael and Andrew. We would all load up in our minivan each night and drive north eleven miles to Ogden, then travel south to Centerville, Bountiful and North Salt Lake to do several janitorial cleaning jobs, five or six nights a week. Tauna and I thought our boys could see where the money was coming from, and develop a good work ethic as they grew up watching and helping Mom and Dad take care of several businesses.

We made the work fun, as we took the boys' favorite Disney videos along with us, to watch in the van on the 9" TV/VCR combo. They watched their movies as we drove to and from our jobs, and even did homework as they got a little older. It was an adventure — like going to the drive-in theater back in the "good old days" when I was growing up in California. Our boys were all bathed and in their pajamas, and were excited for the nightly cartoons they would choose, so it wasn't a bad experience. It was a lot of fun working with Tauna and my boys each night.

We would bring treats, or eat out, and always tried to work and live as Mary Poppins famously stated, "In every job that must be done, there's an element of fun. You *find* the fun, and — SNAP! The job's a game!" We weren't at home in the evenings like most families, but I distinctly remember thinking, *What are we missing on TV, The Roseanne Barr Show?* Ha! Not!!

My mornings were spent either working at another small cleaning job somewhere in Davis County, or just catching up on sleep until my mailman job at 7 am. On the way to work each day, which is less than two miles from our house, I'd see Angel in the parking lot at McDonald's with a hose in his hand. As I passed by in my little red truck, I would honk, — and he'd immediately shoot his free hand up over his head into a big wave, and smile as usual.

It was what would be a continuing pattern throughout his life until we lost him a couple of summers ago. Anytime I saw him at a distance, I got the same reaction and I never tired of it.

After getting a daily wave from Angel each morning, I would see him again a few hours later, as I delivered the mail to his place of work. That would usually be between 9 and 10 am, depending on the mail volume. Again, he was always pleasant, greeting me with his gravelly voice, "*Hola! Daniél! Como te va, mí amigo?*" (Just a simple "Hi Daniel! How's it going, my friend?" Sounds simple and maybe like small talk, but he meant it every time).

On one of these occasions the subject of baseball came

up. As a Cuban, he's obviously a fan of the game, but I wondered if he followed any of the major league teams. "*Claro!*" was his immediate response ("Of course!"). He continued, "In the papers, on TV, everything!" He was a Yankee fan, but that didn't matter a bit to me. I decided one day to invite him to go with me and my family to a minor league baseball game in Ogden to see the Pioneer League Raptors. He was thrilled at the offer.

The Raptors are a team that consists of young ball players who are barely out of high school, and just beginning their professional careers. Most of the players don't make much money, usually a couple hundred dollars per month plus meals, but they have heart and play for the love of the game. They spend long hours on bus rides all over the western United States, with the dream of one day making it to the big leagues. They are affiliated with the Los Angeles Dodgers, the team I followed faithfully in the 1970s. Back then I usually had a radio at my bedside, listening to the games until I drifted off to sleep.

The invitation to see a game would have been for a Friday or Saturday night, (as weeknights were work nights for us). My family went several times with Angel over the years, and on a few occasions we went with my dad, who still spoke beautiful Spanish from his mission in the 1950s. They got a kick out of each other, and became good friends. It was always great to get together and enjoy a few hot dogs and the game we've loved since our youth.

Before that first ball game, all of our interactions were just casual greeting and light conversation, as I mentioned. It was usually nothing more than a momentary greeting. It was only later, at that first game when I was able to spend a few hours with him, that I heard his story and discovered for myself what a remarkable journey his life had been.

I remember that we were sitting on the first base side, up just a little toward right field. We were approximately 100 feet or so from home plate. I always placed us in that general area, either down the left or right-field line, so as to have enough reaction time to protect my young boys from either a line-drive foul ball, or even an errant throw. To every game, I'd bring my baseball glove, as I had been taught by my dad back in L.A. — "just in case."

Dad and I had seen way too many foul balls go into the stands at Dodger Stadium — to EVER think of attending a game without our gloves. Frequently, we'd see a fan reach out with his bare hand to try and make a catch. Not a good idea, when you consider that the pros on the field use a nice leather glove to stop those screaming line drives! Usually the fans just scatter, and wait for the ball to bounce off the empty seats before they race to get it. Or they get the ball that just popped out of the hand of the brave guy who took a stab at it. Man, I always felt bad for that guy.

Anyway, I always watched every pitch to see if a souvenir was coming our way. Again, this was my way of being protective, while also trying to be a hero for the boys by attempting to get a ball each time we went to a game in Salt Lake or Ogden. Over the years we did get several, and one night we even caught two baseballs! We almost had a "hat trick"— three! But the third ball actually bounced off the paper plate I was holding my hot dog and chips on, while my other hand was busy with a Pepsi. I was sort of handcuffed on that one!

*Me and Angel, with Andrew, Michael, Christopher
and my dad at the ball game.
My dad is the smart one up in the shade.*

So that first night with Angel, we were watching the pitcher wind up and throw to a batter early in the game, and I leaned over to my left and casually asked him, "How did you come to this country? Tell me about it."

What he told me was not what I expected, and caused me to miss a pitch. I needed to snap back into an attentive mode to watch for foul balls. What he calmly said was the beginning of the reason why I wrote this whole story — a short account of his life, and ultimately how it changed mine.

I have thought and reflected about what he said for many years. Over time, it's made me realize that Heavenly Father placed a very important and influential person in my life. To my question, Angel kept an eye on the game and looked at me a time or two as he replied that he came from Cuba on a boat that he constructed and that he escaped from the island late one night with seven others.

—"Uh, wait. You made a boat? You're one of the refugees I've heard about and seen on the news over the years??! — Wow, Angel."

In 1973, when I was a ten year old, I always read the daily newspaper to check on the previous night's Dodger game. I always enjoyed an article or two from every page and section, until finally I'd get to my beloved Dodgers and the sports page — and lastly, the comics.

I knew there was a revolution in Cuba before I was born, and I remember seeing several articles about those who would risk life and limb on such an escape attempt. Later, as a teenager I'd watch in disbelief as I saw footage of those brave souls who were escaping persecution and poverty from the islands. Their vessels were seemingly falling apart as the camera crew filmed them in the very moment they were being rescued. They were the lucky ones, as not every story I'd read in the paper or see on TV ended happily.

...And here, I thought, *sitting at my side, eating a hot dog with my family was one of them!* I couldn't believe it, and felt

the emotion rise in my throat, as my respect and admiration for my friend immediately went thru the roof that night, and I told him so.

At that moment, the ball game became a little less interesting, to say the least.

But there was more...

"How big was the boat you made?" I asked.

Every film clip I'd ever seen of these rafts looked like something made out of a weird mix of 55 gallon oil drums, plywood, rope, and sometimes even plastic milk cartons strung together with the little air trapped in them to give the craft an extra bit of buoyancy. Basically it seemed like just about anything they could find in a junkyard, that's how badly they wanted their freedom. *But Angel said he built a boat, and it was for him and seven others, so it was probably pretty big, right?* That's what I was thinking. He missed my question, as he was focused on the game. He continued,"... it was a three-day voyage from Cuba to Florida, a few years before I met you, Daniel."

"Wow! Three days on the ocean, Angel. That's incredible! So, — how big again was the *'lancha'* you came on?" He used the word 'lancha,' which is Spanish for 'boat' — so I was imagining it to be one, maybe like one a Polynesian carves out of wood with outriggers or something. Then he turned thoughtful and looked away from the game for a moment, and slowly said,"It was like 12 feet by 4 feet by 2 feet."

"Wait, *two* feet?" — I was confused. I was thinking of a raft. *What was this?*

"Yes, four of us were going to escape, but eight people came instead, so it was heavier. Therefore, instead of us being out of the water, it came up to here,"as he pointed to the middle of his thigh.

"Wait a minute, Angel! Are you saying that you were straddling your 'boat' as you came here on a three day trip on the ocean? That wasn't a boat you came across the Caribbean Sea...but more like a surfboard!" Wow. The four extra refugees from that impoverished Communist country created such weight on the small craft that it put all eight of them in the water almost up to their waists. This, rather than the original four in the somewhat "safer" position of having most of their legs above the water line as they endeavored to paddle the 90 miles to freedom.

OH MY GOSH.

Think of this scene for a moment: people are chatting nearby about TV stars, celebrities, or maybe what that lady down the street had to say about this or that. We're in a ballpark, with a mid-season minor league baseball game in progress. Perhaps someone struck out, or a pop-up just happened — I don't know — Because sitting next to me is a guy who risked EVERYTHING, including his life — and made it...and now he's the one who waves happily to me, as I pass him while he sprays down the McDonald's parking lot with a hose.

I suddenly felt very humbled to be in his presence. He considers me his friend. I had to swallow hard, and my breathing became difficult, just as it did again as I wrote this sentence.

"Oh, Angel, God has really blessed you. I feel blessed to know you, my good friend!" I choked up a bit. He was composed and unfazed by it all, which kind of surprised me. After having an experience like that, I imagined he would be a little rattled to talk about it. Not Angel.

He replied, "Yeah, three days on the water, just like that."

"What did you do for food, or water?" I immediately asked.

"*Vitaminas, limones, y naranjas*" (Vitamins, limes and oranges). "The vitamins were taken intravenously."

"Wow, you guys were thinking ...very smart."

He went on, "Yeah, one of the guys was medically trained, so the vitamins kept us going."

Then came one of those moments while listening to a foreign language when a word or two is missed — but enough of the phrase or sentence is clear enough to understand.

Here's what happened:

He said one of the guys had an asthma attack, and that he couldn't hold on…(as he was gasping for air) — the way you would, I suppose, if you were at sea on a little craft and without proper medicine, or without your inhaler. I got that part clear enough …

It was his next comment that startled me and caused me to think that perhaps I had misunderstood, or missed something.

He said, "*Se calló al agua y lo comieron los tiburones.*"

"WHAT?! WHAT DID YOU SAY? — SHARKS?!!

He fell into the water and sharks ate him?!! Is that what you said?"

He nodded and said, "Gone."

"Angel!" I exclaimed. This great event in his life now turned tragic and terrible for me in a mere moment's time.

"You…saw a man, taken by…sharks? Wh — what kind?"

…my sentence and my voice trailed off…I was embarrassed as the words formed and came out of my mouth, and I'm still a little ashamed to admit it even now — but it's all that came out. I mean, how do you respond to something like that?

"*Si, tiburones. Eran matios y otros.*" (Yes, sharks. There were hammerheads and others).

I was stunned and totally unprepared for that. You can

only hope that you never hear anything like that in your lifetime, ever.

I regained a bit of composure, and then asked, "Angel, then you had to hold on even tighter to the raft — knowing that there was blood in the water. You were just waiting for another shark attack, right? I mean, your legs were in the water!"

"Yes, we had to hold on the whole time we were afloat. But now it was worse. The water turned red and we were scared, but what could we do? He was lost."

All that was going on around us now, and the game itself, became so unimportant to me. I mean, how do you carry on with a normal evening after hearing THAT?

I don't remember much about that game, but I will never forget the emotions. I just kept thinking: *Wet, sunburned and waiting in ominous terror for a strike from below…or maybe from this side or that…Just so scary…*

Okay, there are lots of ways to leave this mortal existence — but surely this would be the last choice on anyone's list. It's man's universal fear, death at sea by shark. Rich or poor, we all share the same nightmare. But for my friend Angel, it was real.

He saw it up close and personal and had to be thinking, *I'm next.*

"I don't know why they didn't attack us," he said. "They followed us for three days straight, about six feet below the water. We couldn't see them at night" (which probably caused both relief and an intensified fear at the same time).

Can you imagine? Just think about that for a moment, having nowhere to go, with no relief in sight. No rescue. Just you — wet and sunburned, hanging on for dear life, with the overwhelming feelings of anxiety and desperation wearing on your last nerve. The only sound you hear is the water lapping at your thighs and waist, as you alternate between praying, whimpering and panicking for what just might be your very last breath...for three days.

Upon hearing this, I had to breathe and count to ten. I resisted the temptation to demand that all within the sound of my voice hear just what my friend had gone through, but of course I couldn't. I looked around and saw that everyone was caught up in their gossip and the game. I convinced myself that since Angel was able to move on from that experience, and not only survive, but succeed in life and enjoy this ball game, then I should too.

He didn't know it, but Angel taught me a lot about being grateful that night. He was an influence for good, for me and my family in the ensuing years, right up until his death in August of 2013. We stayed close, and went to several more ball games with my dad.

It was fun to listen to them with their different Spanish accents. The two styles were the English equivalent of a Scotsman with a thick brogue and a beach-going surfer from Southern California. Cubans and Puerto Ricans both tend to cut off the last letter in their pronunciation of many words as they speak, especially those words ending in the letter "s." Dad had a clear pronunciation and style of speaking that he learned many years earlier in Mexico.

In 2002, my father was 73 years old, and he continued making the effort to attend my young boys' soccer games on Saturdays at our city parks. He was there with me and my wife in the spring, cheering them on. Then, after a short period of being in and out of the hospital, he passed away on August 20, 2002. He did get to see the Salt Lake Winter Olympic Games in February of that year, which gave me one last series of sports memories with him to cherish.

I'm reminded of those good times every day during the Christmas season, as the lights that formed the Olympic rings high above Salt Lake City now form a large five-pointed star on the hill just a half mile above Kaysville. Each evening at dusk, a generator is filled with several gallons of gasoline which powers the bright lights and reminds the city and passersby on the busy freeway below of the original star and Babe in Bethlehem.

As for my friend Angel, he eventually did get another job in town. It happened when an older gentleman went to McDonald's one day while Angel was working. Gordon Peterson owned the local Kaysville Drugstore. It was an old-time 5 and 10 cent store, the kind that had the welcoming sound of a ringing bell each time a customer walked through the door.

There was also the equally charming sound of flatware, cups and saucers clinking in the back corner of the store, where Gordon also ran a small diner complete with leatherback seats, bar stools and a soda fountain. They made the best garlic cheeseburger, and I would try to make my way there on my days off with my wife, just to be a part of it. Mr. Peterson also owned a couple of apartment buildings. Along with the little white house at 24 East Crestwood that Angel ended up living in, he owned several other businesses.

When Gordon went to McDonald's that day for a burger and fries, my buddy had been cleaning the inside of the restaurant. Angel got after him when an open packet of ketchup fell from Gordon's table onto his freshly mopped floor. Angel pointed out the mess and called him on it. Rather than being upset, Gordon thought it was an admirable testament of the work ethic of a hardworking man, who he just might want to hire himself — which he did on the spot.

After leaving McDonald's, Gordon employed Angel as a laborer on several projects that he was involved in. I would see Angel in various small pick-up trucks, or driving a forklift up and down Main Street, as he went to and from the jobsites, which kept him busy over the next few years.

There was always a smile on Angel's face, no matter when I saw him. Even on the hottest summer days, being from the Caribbean, he was in his element. The heat didn't slow him down a bit. He was always his usual happy self. Our Utah winters didn't seem to bother him either. If he was walking around town all bundled up, I'd get that big wave from him if he heard the horn from my mail truck.

Gordon's kindness to him was limitless. He took Angel under his wing and on fishing trips throughout Utah, which Angel loved to do. As Tom Petty sings, you really *"don't have to live like a refugee."* All it takes is Christian charity. We can't solve the problems in their homeland, but we can serve them while they're here. And the finest example I'll ever see of that is from Gordon Peterson. For over ten years, he provided Angel with a home, friendship and employment.

The Savior Himself memorably said, that when we extend ourselves to others, and care for them in this way, it's as if we had done it unto Him. And who of us wouldn't be honored to do that?

One night on the phone, after Angel's funeral, I was speaking to Gordon about Angel's remarkable life story. He thought it would be a good idea to write it down, and suggested that I should be the one to do it, since he was getting up in years. I agreed that it was a great story, but never saw myself as a writer. It was the first time however, that it occurred to me that perhaps one day I should make the attempt to do so.

Angel is gone now, but not the memory of him. His life is just too incredible to lose to history. Though the details of his life are few, I was positive of this much: he was a freedom-loving hero and a survivor at sea. He was a dear friend, and I would try my best to bring his story to life.

Angel was born in poverty and was raised in Cuba by his mother, along with ten other siblings. He loved his mom dearly, and kept a black and white photo of her in his living room. He had a pair of large hoop earrings, one on each side of her photo, and he'd smile and say, "Look, Momma has her earrings on!"

He had one child, a daughter. I never did learn her name, which I now regret. She is a medical doctor in Cuba, and a part of Fidel's so-called 'amazing socialized medicine' program. "Therefore," Angel said, "she'll never leave." They were able to call each other by telephone on occasion, but being an expatriate, he had no visits with her since leaving the island some twenty years ago.

He was a soldier and served in the Cuban Military. During that time, Angel and the others were instructed by their superiors to keep their eyes on the water's horizon, because "one day the Americans will attack and take away all the wonderful things" the Revolution had supposedly brought to their island nation. Of course, it was just part of Castro's big lie.

So, for the fifteen years Angel served in his homeland's army, they did so. They watched for America's Military Machine and the impending invasion. The battalion believed what they were told, but not all of them. For his last year and a half on the island, Angel and a few of his friends made other plans.

Cuba, the island in the beautiful Caribbean, where 1950s American cars are still kept in running condition because they are dependable and easy to work on, has some of the poorest people in the Western Hemisphere. Since Fidel's revolution in 1959 and the resulting American embargo, things have gone from bad to worse. Initially, Cuba aligned itself with the Soviet Union and received all kinds of economic and military support. After the USSR fell apart in 1989, Russia's financial aid dried up. Since that time, Cubans have lived anything but the Socialist Utopian lifestyle they were promised in the beginning.

The gas they cook their food with is rarely available, so many have resorted to cooking with wood since that time. The food rationing and lack of pay — even in the military, along with everything else being in decline, finally pushed

Angel and the others into action.

Covertly, during their last eighteen months serving in Castro's army, he and a few others were able to seek out and procure specific items they would need to change their lives forever.

They secretly obtained without detection: four wooden pallets, some rope, and the most crucial item needed for their escape: four large truck tire inner tubes.

Think of it: the inner tubes we normally see kids playing with on snowy hillsides for entertainment and fun were the essential pieces needed for their desired plan to leave their homeland.

Since they had to be durable enough for ninety miles of turbulent seas, the tubes would need to be from the large military vehicles they were working with day and night. Clearly, they had to keep this a secret. The fear of detection kept them on the island for another year and a half. They were "playing the game," acting as if nothing was out of the ordinary.

In their hearts, they each had the God-given desire to be free. For those eighteen months, they had to be constantly looking over their shoulders. Living with a poker-face is a dangerous proposition in a totalitarian state. Certain death by execution awaited any Cuban citizen, let alone a military man, if it was discovered that he had plans to leave the island.

Leaving their families was a painful decision for Angel and each of his friends to make, but he had made his choice — and it was for freedom.

He met his three friends at midnight. Each man was to "ride" his own pallet. The four pallets were tied together, end to end, thus forming the "boat" that Angel described to me at that ball game. Each pallet would then have a tire inner-tube secured to the bottom of it with another rope. Tethered together, the four of them would push off, and hopefully make it to America. To his surprise on the planned night of their escape, four additional desperate Cubans showed up to join him, along with the three men he expected. Thus, the weight of four extra people placed them all lower in the water.

With no solid bottom to the craft, or sides for that matter — the seawater continually splashed up through the slats and from every angle during the entire voyage. So there they were: two guys doing a balancing act on each porous pallet, with an inner-tube tied below. Whether the inner-tubes were fully inflated, I don't know. Were they brand new tubes? They were taken from the underfunded military supply, so probably not.

The Quartermaster's books would show what the army did have, and four missing new tubes would not go unnoticed. The four tubes probably came from discarded equipment, meant to be thrown out, perhaps even after having been patched, thus making them unfit for the military's use. That would be the logical explanation for several things, including the long wait to hatch the plan, as they had to search for four tubes which, while not new, were still considered seaworthy.

The difficulties continued, for as they voyaged at sea, one of the tubes lost its air and went flat, leaving that pallet floating on its own, with no buoyancy from below. Without an inflated tube beneath it, a simple wooden pallet would lose all ability to support the weight of one man, let alone two. Angel and his friends probably cut that pallet free. Tied together, the three remaining 4-foot by 4-foot pallets made up their "12-foot boat," with eight men on them — until they lost their one friend Raul.

They remained awake, unable to sleep for those three days and nights, holding on for dear life, to slats of wood, only one-half inch thick by 4-inches wide. They took their vitamins and ate oranges and limes for nourishment. After Raul was lost, Angel said that they were then afraid to relieve themselves in the ocean, for fear of putting anything at all into the water while the sharks followed their every move.

Angel never said that Heavenly intervention was sought through prayer, and though they were part of a Godless society for the past decade-and-a-half, they were all likely raised Catholic. I can't imagine a situation that called for divine assistance more than this one. If there ever was a time for atheists in a foxhole becoming true believers, this would be it.

God was indeed watching out for these remaining seven tired but determined men, for on their third day at sea, the US Coast Guard rescued them from their waterlogged little craft. Instead of the hostility and predicted mistreatment by the United States Military, Angel and his friends were each given a foot-long submarine sandwich, along with what Angel called "the biggest soft drink I had ever seen." He would break into a wide grin every time he told me that part…and I loved it.

He and his companions were each given political asylum. Some went to Florida, while others settled in Texas, California, and Alaska.

My buddy Angel made his way to Las Vegas, Nevada, where he got a job washing dishes in the casinos. It was a job he loved and kept for some time. He felt so lucky to be gainfully employed. Each Friday afternoon he'd be given his weekly pay in cash, which he spent on "beautiful hot dogs" and slot machines. By Monday morning, he'd be broke again and would have to start all over. Now, I'm not condoning such behavior, but to someone who had lived on an impoverished island where many people still cook their meals over burning wood…well…he was making up for lost time. I suppose he felt like he was the luckiest guy in Vegas. He had a steady job and more money than he'd ever seen before. Life was good.

A few years after arriving in the states, Angel made his way to Utah, and to my hometown McDonald's, where I met him hosing down the parking lot. That could be the ending of a very good story right there, and I could wrap it up nicely and put a bow on it — but there is so much more that Heavenly Father has done for Angel and me, that still needs to be told.

There's a line in the 1939 classic film *It's a Wonderful Life* that I'll never forget. Jimmy Stewart's character, George Bailey, is told by an angel named Clarence, that "Each man's life touches so many other lives." It's true. We may never know what effect or influence we have on each other. Well, this much I do know: Angel had an influence for good on my life ever since meeting him, and he continues to do so to this day. I'd love to emulate that gift in my life as well, as I consider it a spiritual gift that Angel had.

So, after all the ball games we saw together under the lights in Salt Lake and Ogden, the years started to come and go with less visits. Angel spent more and more time with Gordon, both working and fishing, which was good for him because it allowed him to learn a little more English. I became busier with my family cleaning business, and with my boys who began having a heavier load of homework as they started junior high. Because of all this, it was only maybe once a year that we were able to get together and go to a game.

With the passing of time, it was only the occasional wave on the street or greeting at the supermarket that we got to chat. This was good practice for me, because he still preferred speaking Spanish, and always did so when we were together. Our visits were always pleasant, and we were able to kind of live off the glow from years past. Ours was a friendship that was sealed from the beginning, and whenever we were together, even for just a few moments, everything felt new again.

A few years ago, Angel began having health problems and retired from work. Gordon continued to let him live rent-free in the little white house, and supported him from day to day. These were two acts of genuine kindness that were virtually unknown to anyone at the time, including me.

I'd still see Angel walking about town when he needed to do some shopping, or just to get some exercise, and he had a few friends who would come to visit him now and then. He looked every bit like a successful, retired Cuban, complete with a flock of chickens in the backyard of his well-kept home. His chickens lived in a free-range atmosphere, with no cages. They too, looked quite happy, scratching about in the dirt for whatever they could find to eat, and they laid five to ten eggs a day for Angel to gather, which he did.

Thankfully, I started seeing him a little more that last year as I'd pass by his house while delivering the mail. Each morning I'd deliver to the local bicycle shop, which was just behind his house, and was only separated from his yard by a chain link fence. Sometimes when I'd make my big U-turn to leave the bike shop, I'd hear a whistle or an occasional shout from him, to get my attention. I'd look up and get a wave from a smiling Angel on the back steps of his house, as he watched his chickens.

After it happened several times, I made a habit of looking for my old friend each day as I left that particular stop. If he wasn't there, I'd continue on and deliver to the bank next door. As I exited the bank's parking lot, I would look to my right at Angel's house, and more often than not, he would be sitting on the little front porch, ready to give me a whistle, a wave, and a smile. Our friendship that last year was maintained in part by his simple gesture. I'd go through my day making my deliveries and not think of him again until later that evening when I'd listen to a ball game.

My summer evenings for the past few years have been spent taking care of a little garden in my back yard. I usually keep busy at least until dark, and to help pass the time, I listen to local ball games on the radio as I work.

The announcer's voice, the pace of the game, and the crack of the bat just sound right on a summer night. The whole feel of it takes me back to my youth, listening to ball games while growing up in Los Angeles in the 1970s.

The Dodgers were perennial contenders for the pennant, and loaded with talent that came from right here in Ogden, Utah. Many of the league's stars got their first professional experience as part of the Ogden Dodgers in 1969. Garvey and Russell, Ferguson along with Buckner, and future Hall of Fame Manager, Tommy Lasorda, were among them.

I digress — my point being that hearing a minor league game over the radio brought back nostalgic feelings as I worked the rows of corn or tomatoes. I doubt I will ever give up that habit of gardening while listening to baseball. In a crazy high-speed world, where grade-schoolers have their own cell phones with internet access, it feels like I'm taking a pleasant step back in time, with the familiar sounds of summers long ago echoing over the yard as the sun slowly goes down. I recommend it to anyone who pines for simpler times.

That's how my last several summers have gone, so when my family comes out and mentions how good our little garden looks, I tell them that God is the Amazing One. He's the one with the miraculous creative power that makes plants and produce out of seeds — I just push dirt around. That's how I see it.

One evening early in the summer of 2013, while working in my garden — Heavenly Father impressed upon my mind that I should visit my friend at his home. It was a strong feeling that I should spend a little quality time with Angel, without the distraction of work. The next day I had the same impression, so I knew it wasn't just a coincidence — I needed to visit him.

The following day after work, I went straight to his house. His little place was built in the 1940s — and yet it had the look and feel of a Latin American home. The dirt driveway had little bits of grass growing in it, and led to a small detached two-car garage out back. The garage had no door, which left a 1960s two-door Corvair with its old black and yellow California license plates looking at you. It was a dilapidated vehicle, with the hood cracked open a bit, making it look like it was going to cough and light up its headlights, and start to talk like in an old cartoon. Still, it looked somewhat inviting, as if there was some untapped potential to it. The rest of the garage went unused for who knows how many years. It was always dark in there, even at mid-day with the large trees bordering his property.

The inside of Angel's house was well-kept and orderly. It smelled clean and everything was in its place. The front room was welcoming, with a sofa for guests to sit on, and a chair for him. There were a few collectibles on a shelf, and that wonderful black and white photo of his mother on one small table. His home had a couple of nice-sized windows in each room. So although it wasn't a big house, it felt quite homey and comfortable. The two large windows in the front room really opened things up, making you feel anything but boxed in.

There was a big TV on the coffee table, and little else in the front room, except for that photo of his mom and a small Cuban flag. He had everything he needed. The little kitchen and laundry area in back of the living room were just as orderly — no clutter anywhere — which is admirable for a bachelor of any age. The back of his home always smelled of fresh laundry. That was always nice and surprising, since there was no woman in the home. There was always a newly-ironed shirt or two hanging on the wall — and windows lined the little room, giving it a bright, country feeling.

All of this and the two bedrooms with the neatly made beds were very impressive. Frankly, I was surprised that a guy so clean and orderly would still be single. I would tell him so, and he would just laugh!

He had welcomed me into his home with a great big hug, as is the Latin tradition among friends. He was so gracious in his demeanor to a guy who had been away for so long. In the past, I'd only been by his house to pick him up for a ball game, so it was a delight to be taken on this little tour of his place.

Even after all these years in America, Angel was still most comfortable conversing in his native language, which was okay with me. It's what we did 99 percent of the time anyway, and I loved hearing him speak his Cuban Spanish, besides being great practice for me. I exclaimed, "Angel! Your home looks great! It's so clean!" For a guy living alone, that's rare. My dad was that way, and it was probably from his military background. Angel seemed to be cut from the same cloth.

After seeing his house and making our way back to the living room, we sat down and I again complimented him on his clean home. He brushed it off by saying, "Oh no, the carpet isn't as clean as I want it. My vacuum doesn't work, see?" He brought his upright vacuum out of the closet, plugged it in and flipped the switch. It wasn't obvious to me that the floor wasn't being cleaned. The motor started to whir and everything seemed fine. He said, "No, no. Look, it's not picking up." Then I noticed a bit of thread on the dark carpet that didn't move.

Since I am a cleaning guy who's been around vacuums for years, I thought I could help. I asked him to turn the vacuum over. I removed the cover plate, and sure enough the beater brush wasn't moving. The vacuum belt was broken. *Thank goodness*, I thought, because this was the extent of my knowledge of vacuum maintenance. I told him I would just get him a new belt, no problem. He said it had been like that for a few weeks, and that he had no idea what was wrong.

He repeatedly thanked me. It felt really good and almost redeeming that after all this time away, I was able to help my old buddy. Our friendship was instantly renewed just like that. It now seemed like no time at all had passed since our last real visit some years before, simply because he was humble enough to tell me about his broken vacuum after I'd been in his home for only a few minutes!

What a guy! He had an innocent demeanor without guile, and I loved being with him. He was overjoyed at the prospect of getting his vacuum fixed. I couldn't imagine an adult being so happy about a vacuum cleaner! After we talked awhile, he invited me to take home the entire bowl of beautiful eggs he had on his kitchen table.

At first I declined, telling him that these were from his chickens, for his meals. He said it was no problem, and that he got several every day out of his yard from his *'gallinas.'* I asked him if he made a big beautiful breakfast with them each morning. To my surprise, he said, "No, I don't like eggs." Ha! This guy is hilarious!!

I couldn't believe it! He said he gives them away to anyone who comes to visit. Wow! I went home with one and a half dozen eggs that day, and was told that when I brought the ceramic bowl back, he would fill it up again for my family.

That weekend I made the biggest, most delicious omelet for Tauna and our boys that we had eaten in a long, long time. Thanks again to my Cuban friend.

I went to two stores before finding the properly-sized belt for his vacuum, and when I returned and put it back together, he was just so happy. Another dozen eggs.

Several days later I stopped back again just to check on his happy progress, and he said, "It still doesn't work." I thought, *What? It was working okay a few days before, when I got my eggs.* I took another look.

I didn't want my small bit of service to be thwarted, and I was really disappointed when, for the first time in over twenty years of working with vacuums, I couldn't even get the bottom cover off to check it out. *What had happened?* I asked Angel if I could please take the whole vacuum to the service shop, and they could fix it for us.

I felt a little embarrassed leaving that day, because I had left him a little less happy than he was on my previous visit, when we thought it was"fixed." I went right over to the vacuum shop and watched, as the serviceman used more than a little effort to finally get the cover off. Before he succeeded in doing so, he gave me a warning that the bottom could actually break with all the extra pressure he was putting on it.

He then said it needed a new beater brush, as somehow the old one had melted to the bottom cover of the vacuum. The entire brush became immobile, even though the motor was working perfectly above. I asked if it could be fixed. He said,"Yes, for about $30 we can get a new brush and salvage the vacuum and make it work."

I believed Angel would definitely like his nearly new vacuum to continue working — so I told the man to fix it, and I would pick it up in a few days. In the meantime, I told Angel that it would be a couple of days and cost about $30 to get it working again. He said he would have a check coming at the end of the week, and could pay for it then.

At this time however, I was actually unaware of his financial situation. I was under the impression that after having worked for his friend Gordon Peterson — that Angel had a small retirement income or Social Security check coming in monthly. He did not. He was living on the good graces of Gordon — rent-free, and perhaps with a small allowance of some kind, but no "check" would actually be coming. I didn't know this at the time, but still wanted to get Angel's vacuum back to him right away.

I returned to the repair shop a few days later, and the owner was kind enough to let me take the vacuum without paying for services rendered. I promised him I would come by shortly as soon as Angel's check arrived. However, I was unable to collect the money from Angel. He kept telling me the money was coming, but after three or more attempts, I finally realized the truth. I was so embarrassed that I didn't put it together sooner. I paid for the repairs myself, and apologized to the shop owner for the three weeks delay.

Not long after, I drove by Angel's house again to make sure the vacuum was in good working order. He invited me in and assured me the vacuum was working great. He even pulled it out for a quick demo, and then we sat and chatted for a few minutes. While we did so, I noticed that his television was on in the background. I commented on a few of the Spanish programs that I would see on my TV from time to time, while flipping through the channels at home.

The grainy picture on Angel's TV screen made me think it was perhaps some far-away foreign station, because it looked like one of the old channels on the UHF band that I remember as a boy.

In the digital age of today this is probably impossible. There are no more fuzzy-pictured programs. All of the Latin channels at my house are received via satellite with crystal-clear reception. I was confused.

"Is that from Mexico or Miami?" I asked. "The picture isn't clear."

"It's from Miami, but the picture's bad because I don't have cable."

"No satellite?"

"No," he replied.

Now I was really puzzled. *How was he receiving any picture at all with no antenna, satellite or cable?*

"Do you know about the little box you can buy for your television that brings in the reception perfectly? You install it, and there are no monthly charges." He had never heard of it.

"I only have this big antenna that someone gave me, from off of a building."

That's when I realized that the only thing that was perhaps "out of place" in his neat front room was this large, gray piece of painted pipe that was sort of leaning-up against the wall behind his big TV screen. I never really noticed it, but now that he mentioned it, I thought maybe it was a piece of exercise equipment. It didn't look like a roof antenna at all.

"Wait a minute! *That's* your antenna?"

"Yeah, but it doesn't work very well. Like I said, I got it off of a building. Someone gave it to me, and I hooked it up to your dad's TV, and these are the only two channels I get."

"Wait — what? My dad's TV?"

Now I felt both oblivious and a little stunned. It was weird to hear him bring up my dad.

"Yes. After he died you gave me his big TV, remember?"

It had been eleven years since my dad's passing in 2002, and we hadn't spoken a lot, but you would think I would have remembered that!

"Wow. That *is* my dad's old set," I said. "Isn't that a TV converter box under it?"

"Yes, but it stopped working two years ago."

"Oh, Angel, if I had only known earlier. I could have fixed it *then*! I'm so sorry."

If I had only visited him earlier, it would be fixed or replaced by now. With the vacuum problem solved, I was even more determined to help him receive the four or five great Spanish stations along with twenty or more English speaking channels that he could receive — free of charge — with a converter box that actually worked! I left Angel and tucked the converter box under my arm, and walked out the door like a man on a mission.

The first step was to check it out at my house. It didn't work, so I went to the local store to purchase one for him. I was told they didn't stock them anymore, since most people had satellite or cable. I was told there was no reason to stock them — you could simply get them on the internet. I looked online, but they were between $49 and $100.

I didn't have that much money, so I called the local Deseret Industries Thrift Store. Actually, I contacted three of them because the first one said that while they did get them from time to time, they sold out quickly. Sometimes they received two or three in one day, but within an hour or two they'd be gone. The manager thought that perhaps people were looking for them in order to resell them online for profit.

I asked, "Really? You think that's where they go?"

"I believe so," was the reply. "But you'd have to be here early Tuesday morning each week to see if another one comes in. Otherwise, it will probably be gone by the time you get here after work."

Oh, great, I thought. *Now Angel will have to wait until I find one of these things, and how long will that take?* I told one of the managers the reason why I needed one, about my friend who made it from Cuba on a raft, and who hasn't had TV reception for two years. I then asked, "Knowing this, could you help me out and save one of these for me when you see one?" No such luck.

However, one store manager did take my phone number and said he would see what he could do. My best option was that in a couple of weeks I'd have a Tuesday off at the Post Office. I continued to look on my own for a used converter box in case no one called me, which they didn't.

A couple weeks later on my Tuesday day off, there were two units available. First thing that morning, I went by, and for $14, I bought them both. I had to make certain that one of them worked and could bring some happiness to my friend. I tried them at home and they both worked.

I went right over, and walked up his steps with the two

converter boxes. Within minutes of walking into his wonderful little home with the just-cleaned smell, we had the first one plugged in and turned on. IT WORKED!!!

My dad's old TV, now probably twenty years old, snapped into crystal clear reception. "Wow! Oh My!" were the first words out of Angel's mouth, and in English!! He was so thrilled. He exhibited unbridled joy, like a child on Christmas morning! And from a 64 year-old man! I was so happy for him!

We set up and programmed his TV with all the available channels, stopping for a few extra moments on the Spanish stations for him just to soak it all in.

"I HAVE TV IN MY OWN LANGUAGE!" he exclaimed.

It was such a simple thing, but it meant the world to him. I can't explain the level of satisfaction that I felt. We parted with a big smile and a hug. I left thinking that between his vacuum and now the TV, I had somehow made up for a bit of lost time. My only regret was that it hadn't happened sooner. However, I remembered that I had acted on that strong prompting when it came, so I reasoned that all was well. He was happy, retired, and the possibilities for good times together in the future seemed endless.

Little did I know that he'd be gone before the end of summer.

About a week went by without seeing him on the street, so I figured he was happy at home catching up on a little TV. I decided to call on him and share a laugh. I got cleaned up after work and went over with my wife, Tauna. She enjoyed his company and he always tried to speak a little more English when he was in her presence.

He greeted us at the door and invited us in. He smiled and said "you're welcome" when she thanked him for the wonderful eggs he had given us. He showed us both how well his vacuum was working, by giving us a little demonstration. I asked him if he would show his home to Tauna, as she was also impressed by his clean and orderly front room.

He took us on a little tour of the place. She complimented him at each turn, which I could tell really made him feel good. He deserved it. Living so tidy on his own all these years was impressive, as it would have been easy to just be a lazy, messy old guy. Not Angel Ochoa. He took pride in his work. The way he kept McDonald's looking new all the time was not a show that he put on just for a paycheck. He was the real deal. He felt blessed, which he surely was.

In Cuba, the loss of real freedoms also meant the loss of economic opportunities as well. Cramped in their small over-crowded government apartments, Cubans yearn for a bit of liberty with no one looking over their shoulder. The lucky ones own a car, even if it's an old one from the 1930s, '40s or '50s. The independence they experience with an automobile is similar to that which the average young American feels when he gets the car keys, only on a much grander scale. They are escaping from the voices, loud music and noise reverberating off the concrete walls of their daily lives.

Coming from an environment like that, where so little means so much, Angel made his humble home a slice of heaven. It was his showplace, where he had achieved the American dream, and you felt admiration for him. His home was modest, as was he — and it made me want to emulate him and the qualities that he possessed.

In his shirt and cut-off jeans, Angel, his presentation and the cleanliness of his place made a great impression on Tauna, who has been my favorite co-worker in the cleaning business since we were married in 1985.

Tauna and I worked together for nine years as custodians at the local LDS meeting houses, trying to make every room look good as new. When she left the Church's employment, she was presented with a little statue of the Sorcerer's animated mop from the Disney classic *Fantasia*. On the wooden base are inscribed the words, "The Queen of Clean." So for

Angel to receive praise from her was high praise indeed. She loves an orderly room, especially if it smells clean, which Angel's did throughout. I felt happy for him again as he received her compliments.

I've been busy over the years at the post office and my little cleaning business. We've made a few good contacts, and have developed lasting relationships. But the Lord really blessed our family with this Angel. I didn't know it at the time as we sat with him for a few minutes, but Heavenly Father was going to bless me through my friend Angel, once again.

As we sat and chatted with him, Angel had his 32-inch TV on in the background. A time or two he pointed to it, again thanking me for helping him. During all of this, a close shot of a shark came up on the screen. There had either been an attack, or a beach closing in Florida, due to shark sightings.

Since it was summertime, when beachgoers flock to the coastline in big numbers, the story didn't seem unusual. We hear of such things occasionally. As I knew of his experience years before on the open sea, I motioned toward the TV screen. He nodded in acknowledgement. I felt I was in a comfortable place, and the situation was right to share something with my friend. After all these years I thought I might mention to him that I, too, had an experience with sharks.

It was only because of the shark on that screen that I felt it would be okay to approach the subject, although I had never previously looked for the opportunity to do so. It was a common thread that he and I shared in life, and this was the first time it had ever dawned on me to bring it up, so I did. I said, "Someday I'll have to tell you my shark story."

I fully expected my comment and the moment to pass. I thought we'd both nod in agreement that "someday" we would get to it. But Angel made a gesture with his hand for me to go on and explain. I didn't expect his response, and realized the task would be a challenge. I had never told this story in Spanish, so this was going to be interesting! I looked at Tauna, sitting next to me on the small couch. I needed reassurance that this was the time and place. She nodded and smiled. I felt that this was my signal to open up about what had happened to me — to both of us, on a beautiful beach in Ventura, California, back in 1987.

I began,"God saved me one day, too, Angel. I owe everything to Him — and to Tauna. She saved me, literally."

She sat quietly and nodded occasionally, as I recounted to my friend the experience that I had thought about nearly every day for the previous 26 years. What happened back then has been a defining moment in my life, to be sure. There is little chance of me hearing a talk in church about God's grace and tender mercies to His children, without my mind going back to that incredible experience.

I definitely cannot get on my knees in prayer, without having the compelling urge to thank my kind Heavenly Father for what miraculously occurred that day at the beach. I had known Angel's story, and he had heard me tell him that his experience was a blessing from God, along with the freedom that was won for both him and his fellow companions. I then proceeded to relate to my friend the experience and great blessing that came our way.

Upon hearing our story, Angel looked at us and said, "Wow. *Fue un milagro*" (It was a miracle).

Angel's place at 24 East Crestwood

54

PART II
Angels Unaware

"Be not forgetful to entertain strangers, for thereby some have entertained angels unawares."

—

Hebrews 13:2

I had been encouraged to write down the whole experience a few times over the years, mostly from family members. "At least" they'd say, "as a journal entry for your family to read some day." I always thought it would be an awfully long journal entry, and I've never been that consistent in writing in it anyway. I leave the family history stuff to Tauna. She's been great at it since we got married. I certainly never considered publishing it. However, this story really was miraculous and I knew it. Like Angel's story, this one also was too good to be lost over time, and after hearing encouragement from my friend to write it down, this time I actually considered it. *Maybe I will.*

Now I'm ready. It's been nearly three years since he passed away, and a little less since the strong promptings I had to tell both his story and mine. So here's what I told Angel:

Tauna and I were both born in the San Fernando Valley, just north of Los Angeles. There was only the hill with the "Hollywood" sign separating our homes from the big city. I spent my first seventeen years there before my family moved to Utah, while Tauna's family left the Valley when she was just two. We met at Bountiful High in 1980, and were married in the Salt Lake Temple in 1985.

Our big day, June 11, 1985

Tauna hadn't visited much of the west coast, and I wanted to show her a few of my favorite sites in Southern California. I also wanted her to see where I grew up, and to find out just how close her house was to mine. We took a two week vacation in February 1987 to do just that. We did the traditional things like going to the beach, seeing Disneyland, the Hollywood Bowl and Walk of Fame among other things. Every day we visited two or three interesting sites, and had a great time and took a bunch of pictures. Driving from her house in Van Nuys to our place in Reseda, we learned that our childhood homes were only about six miles apart in the 100 mile-wide Greater Los Angeles Area. Wow!

We were down to the final day of our trip. We woke up and wanted to go to the beach one more time, but instead of staying in the L.A. area another day, I planned on doing something different.

As a teenager, my friends and I had gone to the beaches closest to the Valley — Zuma and Santa Monica. Tauna and I had just visited those beaches a couple of times over the past two weeks, so I thought it would be fun to cross the county line and find a beach up north in Ventura. By doing so, we would be living out a line from a song on the radio, *Ventura Highway* by the group America. I figured the experience of going up to Ventura would be new and fun for both of us, plus we would be able to check this off our list of places to see, while enjoying one more beach-day before we headed home to Utah later that afternoon.

We drove up Pacific Coast Highway into Ventura County at about ten in the morning. We passed a few beaches as we looked out the window to the west, and figured that any one of them would easily do, so we stopped at the next turn.

Unlike the L.A. County beaches to the south, there were no parking lots or lifeguard towers or crowds — just enough room to pull off the road and park, and enjoy lots of wide-open sand and the Pacific Ocean. After picking out our spot on the empty beach, and with no one else around, we sat and talked briefly. It was only a minute or two before I felt the need to run down and get into that water one last time before our vacation was over.

Tauna liked to tan herself as girls do, so she laid back on the sand as I waded out into the water. It was a beautiful day, blue sky and all. I noticed the waves weren't breaking near the shore as they normally do, so I went out further and further until finally the sand gave way under my feet.

As I did so, the thought crossed my mind that I was going against everything I had ever learned about water safety since I was a cub scout. The Buddy System says to always be with someone, and I was not. I remember thinking, *Man, if my dad saw where I was right now, he would let me have it. Am I really going to do this?* Yes.

Just then, four young guys in their late teens or early

twenties came from out of nowhere, and bounded into the water. I thought, *Wow — that was convenient. I'm not alone. Safety in numbers, right?* I then went out even further and realized that I was a good 200 feet from shore. I remember the waves were still a good fifty feet or more beyond this point, and I needed to be there if I wanted to body surf. With those four guys still about forty feet to my left, I felt like I was somehow connected to them, and therefore felt reassured should I need them for some reason.

So I dove under the next wave that came my way and thought, *Oh, man, does that water feel good!* Initially, it's so cold that it's kind of a burn. The water's too cold for the tub at home, but it feels perfect for body surfing. After the initial "chill" that lasts only a second, you acclimate to it and then it feels comfortable. Like I said, the waves were not too close to shore, nor were they in a regular pattern, as I was accustomed to at other beaches. I treaded water until a big, slow swell came and went. It passed under me and headed to shore without much of a chance of catching it for a ride.

There would be another for sure, so I just waited and made my attempts every now and then. The water was extra flat and calm that day. No white caps to speak of as I looked out further into the ocean. It was so tranquil, — kind of a lazy sea to top off our fun-filled vacation. *That's fine,* I thought. *I'll just soak it in and enjoy.*

I kept my eyes on the guys to my left just to maintain contact, and noticed that I wasn't the only one not having much success with the waves that day. While I wasn't a novice at body surfing, I was no pro either. I began going to the beaches when I was sixteen, and now, at twenty-four, I was only moderately successful at catching a wave.

Here's a little secret: when it comes to catching a wave, it takes timing and effort, as well as a bit of luck. First you have to judge the swells as they come at you, then time your 'kick' by powerfully swimming along with the wave for a moment.

Then, if you're lucky — the wave will pick you up and carry you for a ride. More times than not, (and I mean about sixty percent of the time), you will feel the wave pass under you and leave you behind.

You've seen it in surf movies: It looks like the surfer is going for a wave. He's on his board paddling, and the wave lifts him and his board, and then he just sort of pulls out and lets the wave go. It's not for lack of wanting to take the wave, you can just tell that it's either too weak of a swell to carry you, or your timing was off a bit and you were too slow to go along for the ride. Half the time the water is too weak to carry you, and the other half of the time you just blew it.

Whatever. It's all worth it when you do catch a wave. It's really worth it when you catch several waves on a day's visit at the beach. It's kind of like golfers who suffer through a rough nine holes, but who have the thrill of hitting one or two balls straight down the fairway. That's what keeps you coming back, even when the rest of the day you were in the rough or have a double bogey. So it is with body surfing or board surfing, I suppose. I never had the time or money to do that anyway, but that's what I've heard.

Back to my story:

The morning turned to early afternoon, and I kept my eye on Tauna, who was still working on her perfect tan. Here's the thing — during that last hour out in the water, I knew that soon we'd be leaving for Utah. I kept my eyes alternately on her, the water behind me, and the four guys to my left, in no particular order.

It's kind of like when a student is learning to drive. They are always told to keep their eyes moving from the road ahead, to the rear view mirror, scanning to the left and the right, for obstacles or possible hazards, then repeat. Same thing here: you're always keeping your eyes moving as you tread water out there, looking for a good swell either from behind you, or from your left or right. This I did, along with watching two extra targets…Tauna and those four guys, about every eight to ten seconds.

I knew I had been in the water for a couple hours, and it had to be way past noon. Tauna had changed positions on the sand several times, and my own fatigue from treading water for several hours told me that our time was about up on this great vacation. I thought, *As soon as she gets up off that sand, we're done.*

I knew we'd get our things together and start the half-hour drive back into L.A., and then head over to I-15 toward Las Vegas. We would have so many good memories to talk about on our way home. Happy times and funny stuff, like the night we got caught in the Academy Awards parade of limousines going to Spago's restaurant in Beverly Hills. That was hilarious, as everyone was waving at us in our 1983 beige Plymouth Colt! There was Disneyland and enough photos to fill at least one scrapbook. Tauna was so good at that. The trip was great, and everything had been perfect.

Then it happened.

I looked up and noticed Tauna had changed positions again. She had been on her back with her legs bent at the knees. Now she was on her feet standing, with one arm high over her head, waving in a smooth arc-like motion. It was sort of an *"Ahoy there!"* gesture that you'd imagine someone giving to an approaching vessel at sea.

Mind you, she looked less than a half-inch tall from this distance. I turned to the right a bit, trying to act like I hadn't seen her. It's one of those things that a kid does when he's in the pool, and his mom calls to him that "It's time to come in"— and yet he wants to swim another 5 minutes, or at least until he's told again to get out.

That was my thinking, just to delay for perhaps another moment, the inevitable. I wanted one more thrill. The very moment I turned to my right however, I heard the ten words that I will never forget:

"No, Dan, she's a good wife. It's time to go."

I didn't know if they were words of warning, of admonition, or of a simple fact. They were probably a little of each — but I heard them clear as a bell, above me and to the right. It was very interesting that it was not alarming to me. I wasn't startled in the least. I didn't flinch or look around to find the source from where the voice came. The words were spoken in a calm tone, and were instructive rather than condemning. It felt like a direct, peaceful response to my evasive action of just a moment before when I turned my head — when I hoped for another chance at the water and the waves.

The words and message sounded natural and true enough to me that I immediately began my long swim back to shore. I barely began my stroke with my right arm, when without even leaning forward or arching my left arm out of the water, a powerful wave swept up under me with such speed, volume and energy as I had never felt before. I caught the wave, and yet I had not even completed one full rotation of a swimming stroke. It was effortless.

I caught the perfect wave.

There was, however, no skill utilized on my part in catching that wave. Usually, you need to exert yourself with at least a pretty strong last 'kick' in order to put yourself on the front crest of the cascading wave. The wall of water behind it can then move and lift you forward ahead of all that energy.

There was nothing other than one lazy stroke of what I expected would be a full two minutes or more to get back to shore. At that moment, that wave was, and remains to this day — the single greatest wave of my life. In distance traveled, style, energy, and overall performance, I felt it was the perfect wave. I was being thrust forward at a terrific speed, and everything felt just right. A smooth surface was under and before me, and a perfectly curling wall of water was behind me.

I was just outside of the green room — that tube of water

that forms just before the water falls off the top curve of the wave to the water below. It was spectacular, and felt as if it lasted a good twenty seconds or more, and I rode it at least 100 feet, which is a fabulous sensation.

If you're lucky enough to ride a wave, for even a few seconds, (which can carry you up to twenty or thirty feet) — it is just an indescribably great feeling, especially for a hack like me. This was one wave that I wish my old buddies from my teenage years back in L.A. could have seen. I was full of myself, however, because I didn't catch that wave. *It caught me* — totally by surprise.

Not only did my old friends not see it, no one else did either, except for Tauna.

When the wave finally ran its full course, and had gone far enough to shore so as to not have enough water to keep me afloat — I felt the last of the water crash over my head and turn into beautiful white foam. I shot out of the water with my right fist in the air, triumphant. As I surfaced and came out of all those bubbles and foam, I let out a cry of "Yeeesssss!" I couldn't believe it! It was just sooo right! I shook the water from my head and heard my wife yell out my name, "Dan!!" I turned my attention to her. She had just waved at me a moment before, so I knew she had to be watching.

I'm a bit embarrassed to admit that I was looking for some cheerleading from the sidelines. I motioned to myself somewhat proudly when I saw that she wasn't making any obvious sign of acclamation and thought to myself, *Are you kidding?* Then I yelled out loud, "Did you not see that?" She didn't respond to that, and I didn't hear another word, other than when she called my name.

I had just been infused with a ton of endorphins and self confidence in my abilities. I was still a good 120 feet or more from shore, and thought perhaps there was a chance at another wave, so I turned to my right to see if there were any other incoming swells.

There were no swells whatsoever. What I did see was pretty much what I had seen all day. There was only dark, steel-blue water that was unusually calm and flat, with no whitecaps, and nothing that looked like a pattern of swells.

Only this time, there were two shark fins out there. And from my vantage point — after that great wave — it looked like they were right where I had just been treading water.

Nothing could have startled me more into instantly shaking off my euphoria and forcing me into immediate action.

Several things flashed through my mind:

That's right where I was.

They look only about 40-60 feet behind me to my right.

If they see me, it's two seconds for them to get to me.

Although in survival mode, I realized that I had a moral duty and responsibility to report the situation to my fellow surfers. In one fluid motion my head quickly turned the other way and with my left hand out of the water I thumbed over my head and yelled, "Dudes, time to go!"

I find it interesting that I didn't yell anything about a shark. I didn't want to lose any precious time. Above the sound of the ocean, the wind, and the fun they were having, surprisingly one of the four guys was looking right at me and nodded.

With only a second lost, I took my first stroke of what I now believed would be a long, splashing, panicked attempt to make it to shore. This is exactly what sharks are attracted to and I knew it. I also knew how fast a shark can swim, and believed I would only make it about fifteen feet before I was hit. What a ghastly realization.

I thought, *This is going to be awful.* It didn't just go through my mind, but my entire body also, as I started to swim towards shore. My whole situation *instantly* changed again as I started to swim. Again, only one arm went into the water to form a swimmer's stroke, and, before the other arm came out of the water, a second great wave surprised and lifted me. Once again, the wave came out of nowhere, as I had just looked to my right and had seen the dorsal fins — with no swells or sign of an oncoming wave. Nor was one coming from my left when I had turned to warn the other surfers.

Now, this wave grabbed me and thrust me forward with such a force that I was stunned and almost knocked senseless. Instantly gone from my mind were the cocky, self-congratulatory feelings of my body surfing abilities. I was so amazed at the appearance of this second wave, that even the imminent scare of the shark danger behind me was lost in the moment. I was being pushed and lifted up out of the water, again without any effort on my part whatsoever.

Within a second of the wave grabbing me, I saw that I was not in control and felt dumbstruck. I could only think, *What? — Huh?*

I was confused at the source of the power that was under me. I looked down at the lip of the curl on the wave beneath me as it hurled me forward. The water below me looked and felt smooth as can be, and I was like a perfectly flat stone that had been thrown across a sea of glass.

My body however, was unnaturally perched on that smooth water. Normally, you're in up to your chest, which you utilize as a surfboard with seventy percent of your body submerged as you ride the wave. I saw that I was roughly half-way out of the water, and that I was skimming along on my lower belly — almost to my hips.

At that point, I was on the edge of the law of physics, or defying it altogether. It was as if I had leaned out a window to my hips, with my arms extended like Superman. If someone lifted my feet and legs off the floor behind me, and then let go, that would be a similar sensation to what I felt on that water. It certainly felt different from the first wave, because this time, I was not marveling at my abilities in the slightest.

It was simply amazing to me, that with absolutely zero effort of my own, I was for the second time in just a few moments, taking the ride of my life. It also floored me that once again, this wave was bringing me 100 feet closer to the shore.

A little explanation is in order: When a wave makes its way to land, and if you are riding on that wave, you are not going directly toward the sand, but on an angle. For example, a wave that takes you thirty feet closer to shore might have actually carried you fifty feet or more, (on an angle) towards the beach.

What I do know is this: on back to back waves, I was carried nearly 200 feet closer to shore on the longest twenty to thirty second wonderful rides you can imagine. I was awestruck and felt kind of numb, like how you feel right after a car accident.

I was shocked by the unnatural position of my body on that second wave, and totally confused about where it came from, because it simply wasn't there when I had just looked back a moment before. Also the simple fact that you never, EVER catch two waves in succession.

However, when it finally crashed over my head, I looked up, and was surprised and relieved to see that I was only about thirty feet away from my wife, who stood at the water's edge. I had no time to rejoice in the fact that the second wave took me so close to shore.

I knew my situation was still dangerous, and possibly deadly, so I didn't waste a second by turning my head to check behind me. The reason was twofold: I thought I'd lose precious time needed to get to shore, and I was afraid of what I might see — two fins closing in on me, which might have caused me to freeze up. Nope, I didn't want to do that. I just tried to make those last lunging strokes count.

Then, when I was still waist-high in the water, and my feet finally touched the sand about halfway to shore, I slogged through, in the slow, ridiculous-looking manner many of us have made when horsing around with friends. I wasn't messing around. Some attacks occur in only three feet of water or less.

I was thinking about the back of my legs, hoping that my hamstrings and calves made it out of the water without a last-second attack. Tauna was on the sand, with a stricken look on her face. She was unable to speak — so I didn't know if I had made it to safety yet. High-stepping the last three or four strides to shore, I very thankfully felt the soles of my feet on the sand as I ran into my wife's arms. She was nervous and on her toes, with her hands covering her mouth. I thought they were right behind me.

Thanks to Tauna, and the Lord's grace, I barely made it.

I was out of breath, gasping for air, and coughing up water. I was stunned, dazed and confused. I didn't have my bearings yet — having experienced a cascade of emotions in just over a minute's time: elation, pride, cockiness, excitement, panic and fear, followed by duty, responsibility, and the determination to get ashore…then there was confusion and a numbing sensation, along with the terrifying feeling that this really might be it. I sought to gain understanding as I stammered out her name.

"Tauna," I began, and gasped — "Did you just see that?"

I was trying to catch my breath, my throat still burning from the saltwater, when she lowered her hand from her mouth and said, "Dan, didn't you hear me?"

She sounded scared, almost like she couldn't form a longer sentence.

I shook my head and said "No." I was slightly bending over, still struggling for air. "I just took that first long wave, and after it broke up, I turned and saw those fins. They looked like they were about right where I was —"

"*Dan!*" she yelled, as she pulled a hand away from her forehead.

"They were right behind you!!"

At that moment, my knees buckled and I instantly became nauseous, almost throwing up and dropping to the sand. It really felt like someone kicked the back of my legs, like they do in a junior high prank. I caught myself, and stayed on my feet, but I felt very weak.

"Oh, my..." Now my hand was at my mouth.

Tauna repeatedly took her hands away from her forehead and mouth, finally saying, "I was sound asleep, when something suddenly woke me up. That's when I saw you." She said there were four of them, and I was so far out there, and that she doesn't swim, so she felt helpless.

It was heartbreaking for me to hear her describe this.

Her voice broke when she blurted out, "I saw the fins! They were all around you! I thought I was going to see you go under! I'd be left here on the beach, and I'd have to go find someone and tell them my husband just got eaten by sharks!"

She was near tears, and choking on her words. A real sense of doom enveloped us, and yet genuine relief at the same time. At that moment however, I think the darkness was winning, as we were still shaking and our nerves were raw.

We held each other as we stood there, our eyes locked on the flat water where the two fins were still circling. It was so eerie. *I was out there — right there.*

We were numb for a moment, when off to the right about twenty feet from those fins, we saw another one break the surface, and then another. I was overwhelmed at the realization of how bad a place I had just escaped from. The free fall of emotions sank in. I thought to myself, *Four sharks — it would have been a feeding frenzy. There would have been absolutely no chance of survival.*

"Look! I see a fifth one," Tauna shouted. Then a sixth

dorsal fin appeared, and then another. After several seconds had passed, it looked like there were ten of them!

We were paralyzed in a sad silence, knowing the unspoken odds would have been so far against me. And yet, we were obviously relieved at the same time. Neither one of us moved or could take our eyes off the water. I blinked and tried to shake it off, thinking to myself, *What is the term? Is it a 'school' of sharks, or a 'pod' of sharks?* I mean, I didn't care because I felt safe on the shore, and yet here I was, trying to figure out the correct terminology for what would have been my gory demise. We were freaking out. I mean, we weren't doing some weird nervous dance on the sand, but we were in stunned awe at the sight. It didn't end there.

We exclaimed, "Twenty dorsal fins! No, wait! There's more!"

Then forty or more fins were out there, breaking the surface in an arcing motion. A thought crossed my mind. I was perplexed and said, "Wait a minute — are those dolphins?" Tauna didn't answer and she didn't care, as she dug her fingernails into my arm. She was terrified.

Then nearly 100 fins were in the water. They were getting closer to shore, maybe only 100 feet from us. In a few moments, the number doubled again. Literally 200 or more dorsal fins were in an area that covered about a quarter of an acre. To me it was exciting, an unbelievable sight! All of this marine life just out there. Some were swimming in only 3 feet of water, while others were even closer as the small waves splashed over them in ankle-deep water.

Tauna wasn't having any of it. "Dan, I'm scared!" she said.

I however, was amazed. "They're beaching themselves. How cool is this!" One of the dolphins got nearest to us. It was lying there on its side in only a few inches of water. How interesting as I think back now, that only one of the more than 200 dolphins actually did beach itself. Just this one, and he seemed to be looking right at us.

Gone were the nerves and the queasy stomach I had been feeling before. Strength returned to my legs, and I felt positive again. What a range of emotions, in just over ten minutes' time. I had gone from nearly living out a real-life horror movie to the excitement of child-like discovery. I was beginning to think that this was a fun way to finish our great vacation.

I went closer to the beached dolphin. His mouth was wide open and he seemed to be smiling. He was only fifteen feet from me. I got within ten feet when Tauna, bless her heart, refused to let me get any closer. I was really feeling those fingernails now.

"What if he bites you? Look at those teeth!!"

I looked into the face of the dolphin, and could see that he was actually looking at us.

I said to Tauna, "He looks just like Flipper!"

"Dan, don't go closer!"

I guess I ignored her for a moment, taking one or two more steps. I softly and thoughtfully said, "You come from another world. If you had a message for me, what would it be?"

Only four or five feet separated us now, and I wanted to touch his smooth, gray body, but couldn't, because I was being tugged back by my 100 pound wife.

She reiterated, "No! No, Dan, don't touch it!"

I could see I wasn't going to win this one — so to keep the peace, I backed off.

But it wasn't before that dolphin replied to my question: *"Eeeeeek, Eeeek! Eeek!"* I don't know what he said, but he did say something.

I was just wondering to myself how it all looks deep beneath the waves.

I could still remember paddling in a canoe at the age of eleven, a mile off Catalina Island with the other boy scouts. We could see fifty feet down into the clear water off Emerald Bay. We saw beautiful green kelp, rising up from the ocean floor, the rocks, and large, colored fish... everything.

I recalled all those details, but what I wanted to know from this dolphin was whether it really looked like a scene from *The Little Mermaid*? I was wishing he could describe his life under the sea, but he was probably telling me something else. Maybe one day I'll know.

Tauna and I stepped back, and we continued to marvel on the scene for probably another ten minutes. It was an incredible sight, but we were still alone on that beach. I wanted others to see it.

I ran up the sand towards our car and across the highway to a little surf shop. I knocked on the door, but no one answered. *Probably out surfing somewhere,* I thought. I went next door to the bikini shop, and was glad someone was there. I excitedly told them about the dolphins down at the beach. One of the girls said, "Wow, we're locals and we've never seen anything like that." She and two or three others from the shop returned to the water with me. That was what I wanted, just someone to witness this unbelievable sight.

But wait — I know — what about the four guys who had been with me at the start of the day?

They were in the water with me for several hours. I had yelled a warning to them, but I hadn't seen them since. They now were nowhere to be seen. There was no struggle in the water, and there were no cries for help. There was no offer of gratitude or "thanks man!" at the water's edge when they got out — because they didn't. Lastly, they weren't with us on the sand while we watched the dolphins. They just disappeared. It was just me, Tauna and a few girls.

Within about fifteen minutes, there were others who came and saw. Perhaps a dozen or so stood there on the sand with us, watching. Then, after almost an hour of gazing at the undulating dolphins, we knew it really was time to go and leave this most unforgettable scene.

Before we left though, I wanted to see this from one more vantage point. Just north of us were breakwater rocks, which extended 100 or more feet out to sea. From that point, we could look down and see more dolphins in the deeper water, and it too was an awesome sight.

"Yeah, there were easily 200 of them," we said as we turned and walked back to our little car, and began the long drive home.

That was our experience at the beach in Ventura County, but the story doesn't end there.

A very kind Heavenly Father had other lessons to teach me from that occasion, but not right away. He did it in His own time, and I now believe that He wasn't going to let all that power, grace, and mercy go to waste. His knowledge is infinite. Ours is finite. I had misunderstood *everything* He did for me that day. I still had a lot to learn... and that's okay. Sometimes you've got to learn things twice, before you get it.

We drove home reminiscing about all of our fun, happy memories. We obviously enjoyed all the traditional tourist stops but had almost as much fun at lesser known sites. I took her to the Mexican bazaar on old historic Olvera Street (the oldest street in Los Angeles), the hidden Lake Hollywood in the hills above the famous sign, and everything in between. I know it sounds cliché, but we turned the place upside-down and painted the town red! We saw the wonderful Mormon Battalion Monument which overlooks the entire city, and yet is largely forgotten. We toured NBC Studios in Burbank, and saw a taping of *The Tonight Show* with Johnny Carson. He was on vacation, of course, but Leno was just as good (not really).

We also went by the Walt Disney Studios, which for a guy who grew up believing he was going to be an animator, was an obvious thrill. We took photos at every stop, and saved them in several scrapbooks, along with any small souvenirs we picked up along the way.

Tauna loves scrapbooking and writing in her journal as I mentioned earlier, and she has done so since we were teenagers. Totally old-school in this digital age, and I love it. It's been fun to relive those days, simply by looking at the pictures. The hobby of scrapbooking and sharing memories with actual print photographs, was back in the day before the internet, Facebook, Twitter, and the myriad of other electronic ways kids share every moment of their lives today, ad nauseam.

Believe it or not, there were so many "entertaining" adventures that we had, that the beach story got lost in it all. So later, when we were asked what we did on our vacation, we'd flip open the scrapbook, and point and laugh and comment on all the pictures of us smiling at the camera (i.e. *'Look, here's one of Dan climbing the street sign at Hollywood and Vine'*). Funny, yes, but kind of sad too, because the most important thing that happened on our trip, which clearly changed our lives, was that last day at the beach. By then our camera was empty and packed away, so there are no photos.

The events of that day, however, are etched in our minds.

We only spoke a few times about it, and strangely, it would only come up in certain situations. As I recall, the first occasion was some years later, at the close of a family dinner party. Before the table was cleared, and as a few of us were finishing dessert, my sister-in-law, Lynne brought up what had been on the news that day. She said there had been beach closings on the East Coast, due to shark sightings. This prompted Tauna to turn to me and say, "You ought to tell Lynne and Craig what happened in California."

So there I sat with my plate and water glass half empty before me…and I began to tell the story. Tauna would interject her thoughts, and said that she had been sleeping when it all started. We described it all just as it happened.

As I retold the story, I should have been sensitive to what I was feeling. As I began telling them about that day, the atmosphere in the room was a light and happy one. However, as the story progressed, I remember that when I got to the part about being far from shore…that I began moving my arms as if I were treading water…and I started to get an ominous feeling. There was a definite heaviness in my chest, and my breathing changed as I recalled seeing those fins in the water with me. It once again became very real to me, and always does whenever I retell it.

It often chokes me up. On this first chance to tell the story to my wife's family, I felt the sudden change in my emotions, and the room grew quiet. Everyone felt the grave nature of the situation.

When I got to the part where I questioned, "are those dolphins?" it was as if I was back at the beach, because my mood lightened, and my countenance turned to a smile. I exclaimed, "Man! I'm glad I couldn't hear Tauna yelling to me! If I'd heard her yell *'shark!'* and turned and had seen two, three or four gray fins out there with me, I don't know what I would have done! I probably would have panicked and froze in the water, and been unable to make it back to shore."

I believe I would have been petrified with fear, unable to move. Perhaps like when you hear of a person who is assaulted on a street somewhere in a big city. Even if they believe they are prepared for such a situation, they are scared stiff, and the assailant gets away because he had all the adrenaline.

This is what happened to Police Chief Brody's son in the movie *Jaws*. The boy was knocked into the water and frozen with fear as the scary star of the film swam by.

"Especially that far out," I continued. "Even if they were dolphins, I wouldn't have known it, and it would have just paralyzed me. I don't know what I would have done." I went on, trying to loosen the tension in the room.

"You know how dolphins are supposed to be playful? What if they started coming near me, and knocked me out of the water and into the air like they do with a beach ball in some show at SeaWorld?! If they can kill a shark with a blow to the body, imagine them toying with me until it got rough! Aaagh! I'd still have been a dead man! I was just lucky the waves came and picked me up the way they did."

Tauna ended the conversation on a spiritual note by saying, "It's like the Holy Ghost woke me up." None of us realized just how right she was. My point is that our story ended in smiles and laughter.

"We thought they were sharks, but they were only harmless dolphins!" Ha ha ha!

The scenario occurred more than once this way, and it is the only situation in which the story would come up. We'd be at a gathering with family or friends, and at some point the conversation would turn to sharks. Then Tauna would suggest we tell our story and the whole thing would play out again. In the end, we'd all chuckle and have another taste of dessert, always forgetting the eerie feeling that we all felt moments before. The dolphins always brought a happy ending to the story, but we never came to the truth of the matter — until 1999.

My favorite photograph. Young, innocent faces with their beautiful mom.

Yep, not until a full twelve years later did we learn what really happened. It's not that I needed a dozen years to pray and think about it in order to put it together either. I certainly didn't just shrug it off or pass it off as good luck. I thought about it now and then, but mostly when I was drawn into the retelling of the story.

Over time, my thinking turned to pondering. I wondered, *How did everything happen perfectly the way it did? That was sure lucky.* Then the Spirit prompted me otherwise. I began to learn, as the scriptures teach — "line upon line, here a little and there a little." I found out for myself that we can't get instruction or inspiration until we are prepared to receive it.

When it comes to the Gospel message, missionaries say that some investigators are "golden." They're receptive while reading and praying about the *Book of Mormon* for the first time. Many others need time to study it out in their minds, sometimes over years before the spirit touches them.

It took me years to fully understand the experience we had, and it was not with one *'aha'* moment. Nor was it through my own personal study, intelligence or reasoning that I came to know the truth. It was only because Heavenly Father made manifest just what did occur twelve years before, and He did so in an equally miraculous and incredible way.

First, He gave us the gift of time. Instead of providing us with the answers the next week, or month, or even the next year, He allowed the event to settle in our minds. We didn't forget, but we went on with our lives, and yet continued pondering on what had happened.

In the intervening years, our family experienced some changes. In 1988, we purchased our first home; a condo in Centerville. We fixed it up, inside and out. A nursery room was prepared for a baby. We were ready for our family to grow, but instead, we experienced our first real heartache, due to a miscarriage. We were counseled by friends and ecclesiastic leaders that this was still our child, and that we would be together again one day.

We planned to name him Gabriel, after a sweet little boy I knew on my mission. He was a happy and playful five year old when I met him. He loved the Elders. He'd run around on the grass and throw us the football at the apartment complex. I even looked forward to using his nickname "Gabe" when the time came — but it never did.

Our heartache passed with time, and was later replaced with fulfillment and happiness beyond compare, when in 1990 and 1991, Christopher and Michael were born.

In 1992, we bought our home in Kaysville, a charming old farm house on three-quarters of an acre that had been in the Flint family since the 1850s. We love our home with its big yard and all the trees that provide shade in the summer. Our boys chased butterflies, and loved the fish in the pond. It made for a peaceful, fun upbringing. It felt a bit like Tom Sawyer to us all, as they ran around barefoot. In 1995 our family was complete when our youngest son, Andrew, was born.

We went to Disneyland when they were little, and they loved the Magic Kingdom, as does everyone. We could have easily gone back a few years later, but in 1999 we thought a trip to San Diego was in order. The boys were now ages eight, seven, and three, so we believed a trip down to Sea-World would be educational for their growing minds. Every kid loves animals, dolphins, and killer whales — let alone the sharks they would see. So we planned our trip.

At the time, I had been working as a mailman for five years. The last three were here in Kaysville, working on route two. It's in the very center of the city, and known as "Old Town." It's a great area where I've made a lot of friends, and I continue to serve there, even to this day. There's a beautiful historic home with an old cement horse trough in the front yard, which doubled as the original baptismal font for all of Kaysville over a hundred years ago. I pass by the Tabernacle every day on Center Street, thinking of the pioneers who built it, and tell my wife I want to have my funeral there one day.

We were ready for some time off. I put in my vacation request. As the week for our trip approached, the excitement was building for all of us.

One day, about a week before our vacation, I stopped at a large multiple-unit mailbox. Just as I was opening the door of my vehicle and reached for the mail, a gentleman approached. I had never seen or met him before, so I introduced myself as the regular carrier on the mail route. He just nodded. I told him I wouldn't be working the following week, as we were taking our boys to SeaWorld in San Diego. I told him if he got the wrong mail over the next several days, that it "wouldn't be my fault. Ha!...just kidding!" Then I added, "Yeah, it'll be fun for the boys to get to feed the seals, or dolphins...or maybe even the sharks! They would love that!"

I joked with him that I almost *fed the sharks* as a younger man in Ventura County years before. He obviously didn't know what I meant, so I started to tell him a short version of what happened. Why I'd tell a perfect stranger is unusual, as I'd only told it a few times to family and friends. Maybe it was just to fill the awkward silence as he watched me work. That perhaps, along with the excitement of telling him about our upcoming vacation...and maybe a chance to feed the sharks, instead of them feeding on me!

I placed the many letters and magazines in the slots as I told him the story.

This man was nicely dressed, and had his arms gently folded across his chest the entire time as he stood there listening. He didn't move, nor was there any change in his face or demeanor while I told him the condensed version of what had transpired twelve years earlier.

With no response whatsoever from him, I sort of chuckled and ended it by saying, "So...they were dolphins that I saw — and yet I'd *still* have been freaked out if I'd seen them in the water!... Anyway ..." ...and my voice trailed off.

The man still didn't move, and I was a little uncomfortable by it. Usually, the story elicited at least some kind of reaction, due to the danger — or even a little bit of levity or laughter — something.

That wasn't happening, so as I put the last of the letters in and closed the mailbox door, I concluded by saying, "Yep. That's how it all went down."

Then, something very interesting happened.

He looked at me just for another moment before finally saying, "You saw the fins?" It sounded more like a statement of fact than a question.

Well, at least he broke his silence by saying something, I thought.

I almost laughed. I instantly replied, "Yeah! They were in the water after that first wave. You believe me, right?"

I was still uncomfortable, thinking that the first person who questioned my story was standing before me.

"Yes, I believe you, Dan," he calmly said. I noticed that he still hadn't unfolded his arms, and his body language continued to express doubt.

Then he added, "I'm a student of the ocean, Dan. You saw the fins?"

He finally unfolded his arms and mimicked shark fins with his hands, slowly moving them back and forth. He said, "Sharks always cruise the water. Then you saw the dolphins?"

I couldn't believe he was asking this. I had just described to him what we had seen. "Yes! There were a few, and then tons! Not 50 or 100, it was like 200!" I still didn't get it. *Why was he asking me this?*

"Dan," he said again, "sharks always cruise the water," and he made the shark motion again. Then he added, "Dolphins break the surface of the water," while making both of his hands mimic the action of dorsal fins arching in and out of the water.

He continued, "A few dolphins will scare off a couple of sharks. Those sharks were trailing you. All it would have taken was one of them bumping into you, and it would have been game on. God sent 200 dolphins to scatter those sharks. He sent two perfect waves to carry you safely to shore. He spoke to you, and you *heard* Him, and that's *after* He woke your wife from a deep sleep. You've been laughing at this story for twelve years. I think you owe the Lord a big apology. It's time you know what actually happened."

It's jarring for me to write this — or even to read it — even to this day.

I was humbled, numb, and embarrassed. My knees instantly buckled from behind, just as they had once before on the beach twelve years earlier. I felt the same nausea come over me that I had felt a dozen years earlier, and my eyes became moist. "I need to…um…sit down."

My legs went from feeling strong, to almost dropping me onto the cement sidewalk below. I didn't turn around, but took two steps slowly backwards toward the open door of my vehicle. Knowing that the seat was safely behind me, I collapsed onto it.

My heart pounded and my chest was burning.

I felt the Spirit testify that this man spoke the truth.

He wasn't condescending or lecturing. His tone was even and measured. He was speaking with authority, in an instructive manner, and it hit me and drained me all at once.

I needed to respond, but it took a moment to regain my composure. I thanked him, and reminded him that I would be gone for about a week. He smiled and said goodbye, and I've never seen him since.

I had a difficult time that day, to say the least. My energy was spent after learning the truth. I also felt awful, knowing that I had been making light of it for twelve long years. By mistaking the sharks for dolphins, my story always did end in smiles and laughter, and not as it should have…with the humble, on-my-knees kind of gratitude this miracle deserved.

I had used up a good part of my lunchtime, but it was well worth it. When Tauna came to find me for my break, I quickly told her what the man said. We were both choked up and humbled at the thought that Heavenly Father really did have special plans for us. The two of us were destined to be together, and not just for a short time. We were to raise our boys who would one day serve missions for the Church. They were not yet born when the event occurred, and yet God made it possible.

She said, "Maybe the guys in the water were our sons."

"Tauna, we have three boys."

"Yes Dan, but remember we lost one before Christopher was born."

We were humbled at the thoughts that came to us…

Why did they go body surfing — at that secluded beach — just as I got into the water? They stayed close by me the entire time. When I turned to my left and yelled to them, one of them was already looking right at me.

How is it that after my incredible first ride of about 100 feet on that wave…that they were still only 30 feet to my left? Did they all take the wave with me, thus maintaining their close proximity? That never happens, EVER.

Check out any surf movie. One or two guys catch a wave, and the rest pull out. Sometimes only one guy catches the wave, with the other guys dropping out after only ten feet or more. But there they were, four of them — just playing and treading water, when I looked over my shoulder and gave them my verbal warning.

Then the weirdest thing of all happened, which we didn't realize until just recently.

After I safely reached the shore, and while gasping for air, we looked back at the ocean and only saw those two fins. The panorama was just flat water, with no surfers anywhere. There was no shark attack or cries for help, and on the beach there wasn't a single young man shaking the water out of his hair yelling, "Thanks, Dude!" There was nothing.

We were all alone. It was just us consoling each other. The four young men who had been with me in the water for hours were now nowhere to be seen, and strangely, we were no longer even aware of them. There was no memory of them, and after only a few minutes I began looking for eyewitnesses.

It's difficult to explain, but this part of the narrative is pivotal and very important. We were alert and conscious of our surroundings and the imminent danger I had just escaped from, and yet neither of us made reference to, or were worried about the boys that were in the water with me. It is odd and yet telling. Each time we retold what happened, we included them in the story up to that point — for they were the very reason I stayed in the water at the beginning. And yet, after I was enabled to make it to safety, there was no recollection of them.

We all know the Lord works in mysterious ways.

After I yelled to them in the water, I believe Heavenly Father closed our minds as to their whereabouts, while allowing us to remember them up to that point. How interesting...all these years we've been able to recount in vivid detail everything about that day, yet the memory of those boys — that they did not come to shore with me — was taken from us.

This may sound absurd and seem impossible. With a little reflection however, I've decided that it's not so strange. We've heard that birth "is but a forgetting" of our former life in the pre-existence with Heavenly Father. We have no memory of what was a glorious and beautiful Heavenly Home. However, we know there will be an instant recollection of our life before, and of the loved ones we once knew when we pass through the veil. Therefore, heavenly restoration of memory does occur.

Even Hollywood sometimes gets it right, especially in the old movies. Take for example the 1947 classic film *The Bishop's Wife*. In the closing scenes, Cary Grant, starring as the angel Dudley, informs the Bishop, played by David Niven, that he would have no recollection of him after he leaves. He would not remember being visited by an angel, nor anything at all about the good work they had done together. His memory of it would be erased. Watching the movie, it's the most poignant moment of the film, because the stated message rings true to our eternal spirit: Angels *can* do this.

To the contrary, moviegoers of today are entertained with magical 'Jedi mind tricks.' However, screenwriters of the past worked on a higher spiritual plane, and the public readily received it. The idea on the big screen of a Heavenly Messenger having the authority and ability to erase memory or make one see more clearly, was not beyond the realm of possibility. Where would the idea of having things 'opened up to us' come from? It occurs in scripture.

In the Old Testament, the servant of Elisha had his mind calmed and his eyes opened. An army surrounded him and the prophet by night, and this had made him understandably nervous. He was told by Elisha "they that be with us are more than they that be with them." His mind was then eased as he saw a host of angels and chariots of fire (2 Kings 6:16-17).

Another example is recorded in the New Testament. The Resurrected Lord walked with two of His disciples on the road to Emmaus, and yet they didn't recognize the Master. Although they spoke with Him at length, their eyes were restrained. It wasn't until later that night that their eyes were 'opened' and they knew it was the Savior. Then He was gone (Luke 24:13-31). I always wondered about this story as a boy. *Why could they not recognize Jesus?* They were wise, faithful disciples seeking Him. They were cognizant of the Savior and His mission. *Weren't they worthy to know Him as they were together? Why was it only later that He revealed Himself to them?*

It was only later in life that I learned that the Lord has reasons for withholding the answers to some questions. He does things for wise purposes that we don't understand.

Similar questions came to me over time about us at the beach: *Why didn't we notice that the boys had disappeared? Over the years, why hadn't anyone ever asked us about them?* It's as if everyone else forgets about them in the narrative too.

Again, the Lord does things for wise purposes that we don't understand. Rather than giving us an actual revelation that a series of miracles had occurred, He gave us the gift of *time* — *time* enough to replay it in our minds, *time* for Him to reveal "here a little and there a little," *time* to pray about it and to give thanks for what we did know. Perhaps that leads to more discovery — like peeling layers off an onion. Who knows? Maybe it would have been way too much to have known just how many miracles took place that day, and all at once.

I now believe it wasn't because of human frailty or weakness that we didn't figure this out the day it happened. I believe it was by design. It was a wise Heavenly Father who knew it would be best for us to learn and appreciate it slowly, day by day. He even says in scripture, "Behold, ye are little children and ye cannot bear all things now; ye must grow in grace and in the knowledge of the truth" (D&C 50:40).

Had the four young men made it to shore as I did — all out of breath, fatigued and grateful to be on terra firma, one would expect that they would have joined us, thanked us, and given us a "high-five." No doubt the six of us would have discussed the shark fins, the dolphins, and everything that transpired. I definitely wouldn't have gone looking for other witnesses, as we would have had an instant camaraderie with these four.

I believe this is how it happens in such instances. For example, after a car accident, bystanders tend to gather and talk amongst themselves about what they just witnessed. Strangers, only moments before, now seem like friends due to the shared experience. Certainly, a near shark attack among five men in the water would have brought us together.

I've had many years to think these things over. But initially, we were just stunned by the new revelation from this man who just came and went. All of this came to my mind after I told Tauna about the stranger on my route.

I showed her how he explained the difference between the dorsal fins with his hands. She looked away in a stare and nodded, saying, "Yep, the fins were crisscrossing, and stayed above the water. Those were sharks. It wasn't until the other fins appeared that they went in and out of the water, the way dolphins do."

Like something right out of scripture, our eyes were opened. While for years we understood only in part, because of this messenger, we now knew the whole truth.

Later that night, we did as I was encouraged to do, and knelt together in prayer. We thanked Heavenly Father for revealing what had happened so many years before, and apologized to Him for not recognizing the miraculous blessing He had given to our family. Lastly, we acknowledged our embarrassment for having 'laughed at it' for years.

The next morning, I arose from my bed and wondered what to do next.

Throughout history, non-believers, doubters, and the faithless have asked prophets for evidence of the Divine. The Savior Himself was challenged occasionally for "some kind of a sign," as was the case with Herod, but He refused them.

During my teenage years, I began thinking more about religion, and at times I thought, *Gee, it would be so neat to witness something spectacular, like a miracle out of the scriptures. Then I would believe, without any doubt at all.* How juvenile — just like King Herod himself.

Looking back, I'm embarrassed to say that I wasn't much different than the sign seekers. It's human nature, I guess. As fallen man, it's likely that many if not all have hoped for the same type of thing. Still, that's no excuse — as I've since learned that it's an unrighteous desire.

I now recognize many years later, that something very miraculous *did* happen in my life. I was a common man, a custodian and caretaker at one of the Lord's meetinghouses, and yet I was blessed to experience a miracle of biblical proportions.

I know for a fact that I was saved and preserved like Daniel in the Lion's Den — only I was in water, surrounded by sharks. *Could their mouths also have been shut, as it happened in the biblical story* (Daniel 6:22)? *Had the dolphins been 'prepared' by the Lord as it happened to the great fish in the story of Jonah* (Jonah 1:17)? I wondered. *Were they kept at bay by an unseen angel? Or did they hear the voice of their Creator, or that of His messengers?*

Perhaps they were held back until the dolphins came, or at least until those two incredible waves came and carried me from imminent danger.

Also, those four young men; were they His messengers? I have always wondered about them, as well as Tauna's sudden awakening on the beach. Finally, those ten distinct words that I clearly heard all those years ago, which have never left me: *"No, Dan, she's a good wife. It's time to go."*

If I hadn't listened, I would have lost her.

How blessed I was on that day, and continue to be. He was my Deliverer — no different from Daniel in the days of old — and I'll always praise Him for it. I'll never wonder or doubt again, for I know for certain that there is a Living and very Loving Heavenly Father — who does indeed know us all. I continue to ask for His help each day, but I certainly don't ask for signs or evidence. I feel He has already given me my life's allotment of divine assistance.

In the New Testament it says "your Father knoweth what things ye have need of, before ye ask Him" (Matthew 6:8). For those who seek God, yet still wonder if He *really* has time to be concerned about us, the Apostle Paul beautifully states: "if any man love God, the same is known of Him"(1 Corinthians 8:3). I came to know this is true, He really does know us!

In one of his films, it was the great American actor and patriot John Wayne who said, "Life is tough, but it's tougher if you're stupid."

Right on, Duke!

I was given this huge blessing, and almost missed it. I know that sounds pretty stupid.

Let me just say that life has gotten easier since learning what He did for my family. Life still has its challenges and can be tough. That's the way it's supposed to be, by design. John Wayne was right, it would have been even tougher if I had been stupid and brushed it all aside, ignoring Heavenly Father, and believing I made it to safety on my own.

I was only twenty- four when it happened, and relatively young at thirty-six when it was revealed to me what had actually occurred. I believe now that the entire matter was in Heavenly Father's hands. It was in His time frame that we learned the truth. Therefore, it wasn't that we were being naïve, or dumb for not understanding from the beginning. This experience has taught me that He gives us the time which allows us to gain wisdom and maturity on matters to a degree or level that wouldn't develop otherwise.

I recently heard the saying,"In youth we learn, and with

age we understand." This has given me a measure of great comfort. We spend many of our early years learning, both academically and in Sunday school. As young adults and even as married young couples with children, we're really just beginning to learn the spiritual things of eternity.

In the New Testament, Jesus taught in parables, which we've been told were used for two reasons. His stories were about everyday life, that they may be easily understood. And yet, the key to the lesson was sometimes hidden, so as to cause thought, reasoning, and reflection on the part of the hearer, in order to reveal an even deeper meaning.

Similarly, we should be thinking about the blessings Heavenly Father has given us, in order to find the deeper meaning.

A great example of this kind of thinking is found in the life of Mary, the mother of Jesus. After experiencing the angelic annunciation, she was afforded time to reflect again and again on the great event which was to come. After His miraculous birth in Bethlehem, it's important for us to remember and learn not only from the Savior, but from His dear mother as well, as she "kept all these things, and pondered them in her heart"(Luke 2:19). I believe she did this throughout her life.

Pondering may be a bit overlooked these days. Some things cross our mind, we may think things over, but there are only so many hours in a day. With the endless stream of information on our hand-held electronic devices and computer screens, let alone TV, radio and video games, much of our quiet or reflective time has been lost. This is tragic and a huge waste of our time. We would do well to learn from this chosen vessel, who was "blessed among women."

Patriarchal blessings are Heavenly manifestations, available to all members of His church, and are worthy of such consideration. These are the great things in our lives which should find frequent place in our thoughts, as it was with the mother of our Savior. I'm over a half-century old and still read mine that I received in 1983, to see what I might do to realize the promised blessings.

Gifts or blessings which are appreciated now, can also appreciate in number. As the scripture states, "he that receiveth light, and continueth in God, receiveth more light" (D&C 50:24). Those who gratefully recognize His hand in their lives are apt to receive more. We should continuously be giving thanks to the Giver of all good gifts which come from above (James 1:17).

One example of a temporal blessing which appreciates over time is a trust fund, established by parents, for their children. Usually in this earthly gift, funds set aside cannot be accessed until the beneficiary reaches a certain age, sometimes even to the age of thirty or more. This is done for an important reason. Individuals in their twenties or younger may not be mature enough to handle that great responsibility. In fact, they never are, because I was twenty once!

Perhaps Heavenly Father sees the same in us. Often it is through the passing of time that He reveals the meaning of lessons in our lives. It may not be until years later before we realize, *Oh, that's why it happened.* We read that the passing of time was even a blessing in the life of Jesus, as He learned and grew 'from grace to grace' over time.

The passage of time has been a blessing in my life, as I've had nearly thirty years to think about that day on the beach. It has changed my way of thinking, and definitely my prayers.

I've been able to move forward and go about my daily life, and although it isn't in the forefront of my thoughts, not a day goes by that it doesn't cross my mind. My testimony has been strengthened because of all He has done for me. I am comforted every day, knowing that He loves me, and I sleep well each night. But it wasn't always that way.

After returning home from our San Diego vacation in 1999, there was a period of about two months when it was very difficult to get a good night's rest. I couldn't shake what the man told me concerning the sharks. I'd have a great day, going about my business and not worrying about it at all, only to awaken at 1:30 in the morning in a panic.

I repeatedly dreamed that I was back in the water, experiencing the worst. Every night I relived the entire episode, from every angle imaginable. I would see the head of a great shark as it came at me, from the right or the left. Sometimes I'd see the fins coming at me from a distance, and I'd awaken in a cold sweat. Talk about your worst nightmares, over and over.

The Wall Street Journal recently ran an article which named the three things that are man's greatest primal fears. They were falling, being eaten, and dying from asphyxiation. When I read that, I immediately thought of my sleepless nights from several years ago. I realized that in my reoccurring dreams, I was experiencing all three of these fears on a nightly basis. I was being eaten alive, drowning, and then falling to the ocean floor. Oh, what horrible nightmares they were, and they haunted me.

Consider this: When you are treading water, you are fully submerged to your shoulders. Therefore, in my dreams the rest of my body was dangling like a five foot long piece of bait. Each night as the dream unfolded, the sheet from my toes to my chest felt as if it were the water. At some point I would see one or two large dorsal fins approaching. In a nightmare or in real life, if you ever find yourself in that situation, there is no magical way out. You're on your own.

I know it is said that you can drive a shark away by hitting it in the eye, and that would be the obvious first and last resort in case of an attack. Many have had success with that method, but to me it seems like you'd be punching something the size of a refrigerator as it moves by with the intent of taking one of your limbs off. Oh yeah, one more thing: he can see and breathe under water and you can't. Good luck with that.

First of all, the size of your fist means nothing if he sees it coming and that mouth is open. If he wants you, it's all up to him. You're on the menu if he's in the mood, and you have little or no say in the matter, especially if several of his pals have come for dinner. Then it's a feeding frenzy, and it's over in the first round. I'm not trying to be a fatalist. I'm just amazed every time I hear or read about survivors of shark attacks. In most survival stories, it seems there are others close by who are able to give aid or help the victim get to shore immediately after the attack.

My dreams never ended that way. Sometimes I'd even see Tauna far off on the sand, and I'd look up to her, and just from the look on her face, I knew it was "goodbye." Every night I'd wake up at the very moment of being hit. Sometimes I'd only wake up after being dragged under water at a high rate of speed, with bubbles and varying shades of blue-green water swirling around me, mixed with my own blood. In that version of the dream, I think I'm never going to make it back to the surface for another breath of air. Again, with no chance of survival.

It was awful, with one particular three week period being the hardest. I remember it was night after night without any rest. I'd awaken with my legs involuntarily pulling up under me in the bed, trying to keep away from what I thought was just beneath me. It was shocking to my senses, and night after night it felt like I was having a heart attack.

Many of us have dreamed of running away from something, and we laugh and make jokes about it. Now just imagine that your dream is so vivid, that you awaken and you are actually running. That's how real it was, with my legs shooting up under me, causing me to awaken in a start. As I mentioned, the sheets on top and under me felt as though they were the water. This gave me the added physical sensation of actually being there again, to go along with the images flashing uncontrollably in my mind.

After awaking up, I never could go back to sleep. Night after night I'd see these gray fins coming at me, and all I could do is wonder — *is it a great white, a blue, a tiger shark, or a hammerhead?* I could only guess after I saw their faces in the water — about two feet from me, but when they're that close it's too late anyway.

Sometimes they'd breach the water, as seen on the Discovery Channel's *Shark Week*. I'd get knocked out of the water like a car had hit me from beneath.

It was just terrifying. Besides losing sleep, I was also waking Tauna night after night. Sleep deprivation was setting in, as I could feel it throughout the following days and weeks.

Desperate and not knowing what to do after several weeks, I called my dad in California. Years earlier, he told me that it would be okay to call him at any hour, any night I had a problem or concern. I had done so a few times several years before, and each time he answered the phone and calmly helped me with whatever it was that troubled me. I always apologized for interrupting his sleep, but he told me it was not a problem, and that he could get right back to sleep. He'd tell me that he was glad that I could depend on him, even in the middle of the night.

He knew the shark story from twelve years earlier, but now was surprised to hear that I was unable to sleep because of it. I told him that my dreams kept repeating the horrible details of what could have happened. I mentioned that I was going to work each day on only a few hours' sleep, and that it was becoming increasingly difficult.

He listened and realized that it had developed into a real problem. He gathered his thoughts and said, "Dan, you need to tell yourself, — that none of it happened like that. You were protected, and God preserved you. Pray for help, you can do this."

I said, "Dad, I have prayed. Tauna tries to calm me down, but I just can't sleep. It just keeps coming back every night."

He reassured me, and told me that I had overcome the great odds that were against me in the water. He said that God saved me, and that I could overcome this too, with the Lord's help. He is the One who helped me back in 1987, and He would help me again.

He was right. The phone call ended, and I rolled out of bed. I knelt and again thanked my Heavenly Father, this time bolstered by my dad's words of encouragement. I then told Him of all that had happened recently. I was afraid that my learning the truth would all be for naught if I had trouble at work due to lack of sleep. I asked for it to end so that I could get the rest I needed for the following day's work. Thankfully, the nightmares ended that night.

This time, He saved my health and sanity so I could earn a living for my family.

In the many years since then, I have reflected on the entire series of events as one big episode. Over the span of a dozen years, He preserved me, kept me alive, and used others to teach me one long lesson. It may sound unusual to need twelve years to learn from something so powerful, in an age when kids hold the internet in their hands.

I'm one of the last living dinosaurs that still doesn't understand today's technology. I'm an old- fashioned mailman. I keep reminding myself that the Postal Service was once high-tech stuff too — in the 1800s! Happily for me, most of the customers on my route would rather get a hand-written Christmas card rather than an E-card, and I'm with them.

Today's world is seemingly addicted to instant gratification of the electronic kind. If it's not put in 134 characters or less on a hand-held cellular phone, it's taking too long.

"Gotta move on to the next thing"…"Gotta check my phone for messages"…"Gotta update my social network pages and check my e-mails." It's the sort of thing that requires us to be in constant contact, with someone — anyone …endlessly streaming information. This high-speed lifestyle has made some smart people go "off the grid." They pay good money to go on vacation without any electronic devices or phones, just to disconnect from it all.

There's another way, a cheaper way — to enjoy quiet time away from the world, and it's the Lord's Way. Since the beginning, He has wanted us to make time to reflect on the important things, without all the hurry. We need time for prayer and reflection. Even doing so as we drive without the radio on is beneficial. A little quiet time is good, and quickly adds up to our benefit.

Consider our Temple worship. We learn a little every time we serve in the House of the Lord. We don't just go once and think, *Been there, done that.* We gain a deeper understanding of the promises and blessings with each visit. We are not expected to hear and fully comprehend everything, like we do when we read the box score in the sports page from last night's game.

We can learn "line upon line, precept upon precept," as the scriptures say. He even promises... "if thou wilt inquire, thou shalt know mysteries which are great and marvelous..." (D&C 6:11). I believe some of these mysteries may be the events of our own lives.

A few years ago, a high councilman stated that "we learn things retrospectively, and not prospectively." It was a talk that definitely caught my attention, as it made me think of this event in my life, and how I've learned from it, looking back over the years.

I had to agree. I believe we learn much when we look back. I certainly didn't understand my situation fully while in the water that day, but over time, the Lord revealed to me what a great and marvelous thing He brought about. His is a church of continuing personal revelation. Of this I have an unshakable testimony.

PART III

Angels Among Us

*"...I will be on your right hand and on your left...
and mine angels round about you, to bear you up."*

—

Doctrine and Covenants 84:88

Through this singular experience, I've come to know for myself that Heavenly Father doesn't do great things only for the chosen few. I've been familiar with the scripture since Primary that states: "God is no respecter of persons" (Acts 10:34). Now though, it has personal meaning.

When Moses led the Children of Israel to the Red Sea and parted the waters, it wasn't just for God's prophet and his brother Aaron. Approximately two million men, women and children experienced God's great miracle.

Therefore, it wasn't just for the scholars, academics or the privileged, but for every-day, average people like you and me. They also witnessed the many powerful miracles in Egypt, before Pharaoh finally let them go. Each one of these miracles was awe-inspiring, and strengthened the multitudes' faith in the God of Israel. Then He saved the best for last. Fleeing 600 years of bondage in Egypt, they experienced the incredible and terrifying sight of millions of gallons of water on their left hand and right, as they traversed the midst of the Red Sea on dry ground. Each individual soul witnessed God's power and might.

There were others who saw the miracles of Heavenly Father, or of His Son, Jesus Christ. On one well-known occasion, He fed five thousand in the desert. Soon after, at the Sea of Galilee, He performed the same miracle, feeding another four thousand. He also blessed countless numbers of sick and afflicted souls, both in the Old World and in the Americas. He also did many miracles through His prophets. The vast majority of those were done for the benefit and blessing of the unheralded common man, like you and me.

One of my personal favorite miracles that the masses were permitted to witness was from the Old Testament. All of Israel was on Mount Carmel to watch, as the prophet Elijah challenged the 450 priests of Baal along with 400 other false prophets to a dual, to see whose God is God. One man against nearly a thousand (1 Kings 18:19-39). Guess who won!

What a sight that would have been!

These are a few examples of the many who were eyewitnesses of His almighty power. Regular everyday people — again — just like you and me.

After seeing with their own eyes, each of these individuals still had a life to live, full of opportunities, challenges, and difficulties. Being a witness to God's great miracles did not make them or their lives perfect. We know there is only one Perfect One.

The same is true for me. The only way I'm "perfect" is that I'm perfectly flawed.

I learned that from none other than Ted Nugent, the musician. He made that comment about himself during a radio interview that I heard several years ago, and I've never forgotten it.

I've stumbled along these many years, and occasionally fallen flat on my face. I try to do my best, yet I know that I've come up short and have great need for the Savior.

I need Him, I depend on Him, and I love Him. He is my only real hope in life. Without Him, I'm just spinning my wheels.

I recognize that this whole experience has been nearly

three decades long, and though it's taken that much time, it hasn't lessened the value of His saving grace and mercy that He has shown me. It is priceless beyond measure.

Have I had problems or challenges since that day? Certainly. Does it occasionally feel like I'm still in deep water with danger just below the surface? Absolutely. Do I still plead for His help, sometimes many times a day, feeling like I'm on my last leg? Regularly. Through the many challenges in my life, I remember that which He has *already* done for me, and this brings me comfort and peace of mind that He's watching.

A little over two years ago, I began writing about my friend Angel, how our lives intersected, and how we learned that we were both preserved at sea. As his story of survival blended into that of my own, I *wondered* just how many great things did the Lord do for me in order to enable me to safely get to shore that day?

I realized it wasn't just one miracle, but many. And so I started counting.

First, He blessed me with those four young men. They could have chosen to body surf anywhere along the California coastline that day in February 1987. Instead, they came along just as I waded out into the water and wondered to myself, *Should I be out here all alone like this?* They gave me comfort and assurance that I wasn't alone.

He blessed me, and I cannot stress this enough — that I did NOT see the fins all around me in the water. Recently I asked Tauna if she only saw fins behind me, and not to my left or my right (I've often wondered how they stayed out of my peripheral vision). *Did they only surface at my right when I was looking to my left, and vice-versa?* Tauna's answer shocked me. She said, "They were circling you." She didn't realize I didn't know. I am so grateful that I did not see them. I was preserved by *not* seeing, and therefore *not* panicking until the situation was resolved.

Tauna was suddenly awakened from her deep sun-induced sleep, and alerted to the danger by the Holy Ghost.

I then was blessed by not hearing her screams of *"Shark!"* If I had, I would have been paralyzed with fear.

I was highly blessed and privileged to hear the softly-spoken words, *"No, Dan, she's a good wife. It's time to go."* I heard that divine instructive voice audibly, and yet I couldn't hear her high-pitched, panicked call of warning.

He then sent a perfect wave to carry me from danger, and quite possibly at the very last moment, for after I rode that wave and looked back, they were right there. Now, God is the creator of heaven and earth. Everything He created knows His voice and obeys. When the waters of the Red Sea parted, the very elements obeyed His voice through His prophet, causing an immense body of water to rise up and move out of the way of the children of Israel. I'm not putting my experience on the same level as that great event, but I am saying…that there was a powerful energy in the thrust of that wave. It *felt* different. It was palpable, and it was even more evident on the second wave than the first.

Then He sent a second wave, more powerful than the previous one. This never happens, certainly not two waves in a row that are worthy of a movie. I barely had time to recover from the first one, when the second wave picked me up and carried me at least another 100 feet closer to safety. I was moving along on that wave whether I wanted to or not, with my arms completely out of the water. I was in an unnatural position, and spent the entire ride looking down in bewilderment and disbelief.

He sent dolphins. Lots and lots of them. *Were they keeping the sharks at bay below? Did they or angels keep the jaws of the sharks from me, like in the story of Daniel in the Lion's Den?* The sight of the dolphins eased our fears, only seconds after being sickened at the thought of being torn apart before my wife's eyes.

A full twelve years later, He sent a messenger out of the blue. Someone I had never met before, and haven't seen since — to declare with words of soberness, the truth of what actually happened that day. Because of this, I nearly collapsed. Like Daniel in the days of Nebuchadnezzar, I believe God revealed His secret to me of what really occurred.

Then, several years later — one more last great blessing came my way:

I was sitting in church when a speaker from the pulpit read the familiar verse from Doctrine and Covenants 84:88, *"I will be on your right hand and on your left...and mine angels round about you, to bear you up."* This time however, the hair on the back of my neck stood up, and my skin tingled. I had an overwhelming confirmation from the Holy Ghost that this is indeed what had occurred.

He literally lifted me from the water on that second wave. I remember having to look down to see just how much of me was still in the water. It was stunning. I believe that was why my underarms felt awkward as I raced along the water toward the shore. I wasn't even using my arms, as I did on the first wave. Instead of my arms being forward, they were out of the water, elbows up.

Sitting there in church, I felt a distinct burning in my chest, and it all became very clear to me, as my eyes filled with tears. I didn't hear anything else the speaker said, as everything became a blur. Dressed in my white shirt and tie, I realized at that moment that I just learned a little more. *"Line upon line, here a little and there a little."* That was very humbling and overwhelming, as the Spirit whispered to me of what had happened so many years before. I quickly grabbed my scriptures and reread the verse. Again, there was a huge burning in my upper chest. I had my answer. There *were* unseen angels helping me that day.

We've been taught over the years to 'liken the scriptures unto ourselves,' and this whole series of events in my life has been one long exercise in doing just that. I can clearly see that the Lord has been present in my life, and I know that I have been preserved.

Since that time He has allowed me to become the father of three great boys, with whom their mother and I have shared countless great memories, and a few special spiritual experiences. We've been blessed to raise them in the light of the Gospel. Through this experience that their mother and I have shared with them, our sons have a sure knowledge that there is a God in Heaven, powerful and almighty to save, in every sense of the word. He is our Father in Heaven. He is loving, and so very caring — enough so as to reach out in a mighty way to save even those of His children who are lowly in station.

He loves us all equally from the greatest to the least. It may sound like boasting, but how can I say too much about my Heavenly Father, who has done such an incredible thing in my life? Alma 26:35-37 speaks of just such an instance. *I'm boasting of Him, not of myself!* I know that He exists and that He is involved in the lives of His children. I've heard about it, read about it, and now lived it in the most vivid way imaginable.

So now I'm going to declare it, come what may. I've pondered on this event in my life for nearly three decades. I am eternally grateful for what He did for me and my family, and will feel the same way one hundred years from now. I also feel He did it to save Tauna. I believe He loved her, so He saved me. Having lost her dear father at the young age of seventeen, she did not need to witness an awful scene at the beach and be made a widow at the age of twenty-two.

Had the worst happened, she would have had to stagger up the sand to find help on her own. That would have been very difficult for anyone. I believe it was her goodness, and her life that merited such a miracle as this. After all, she was the one the Spirit first alerted to the awful danger in the water. Without her wake-up call, I'd have actually lived the nightmare that kept me up so many nights years later.

I told her then and still tell her to this day, "God saved me... because of you."

When we were teenagers, she was my dance partner in the awesome eighties, and has been my business partner and eternal companion since then. She's a cancer survivor and an amazing woman. I know I couldn't begin to do four jobs a day without her, let alone raise three fine sons. She's a helpmeet in every sense of the word, and we just celebrated thirty-one years of marriage together this past June. I love her to bits, and I can't imagine my life without her. She's my lifesaver, and I owe everything to her.

I feel it is true, that if I had not done the right thing, and INSTANTLY began swimming just after hearing those ten words...I might not have made it. I believe it was like the scripture in the *Book of Mormon* which says that it is "by grace that we are saved, after all we can do." I had to put forth my puny effort, as small and meager as that first stroke was, or I would have missed the wave and my opportunity for a great blessing. It was just enough, and He did the rest.

Over the years, our boys have heard us tell the story of what happened that day, and yet we thought that someday we should put it down on paper, when the time was right. We wanted to do justice to a life-saving experience that was both marvelous and miraculous.

When the time was right.

Isaac Watts was a seventeenth century Christian who wrote more than 600 songs in his lifetime. He penned the familiar *"He Died! The Great Redeemer Died."* The beautiful third verse begins with these words: "Here's love...beyond degree." When we sang this in a recent Sacrament Meeting, I again felt the Spirit touch me as it did years ago, confirming to me that I was helped by angels. 'Love beyond degree' was exactly what was shown by Heavenly Father to our family. It *was* beyond degree.

So I decided it was time.

Above all, I would need to make one thing clear — it was only due to His power, mercy and saving grace that I made it to shore, and lived to tell about it.

I'm so grateful to be their father. It's funny, they like to tease me when I don't remember the details of the latest movie that they were so excited for us to see just weeks before. That's okay, because I still have the events from 1987 firmly etched in my mind. To me, that's what is really important, because it lets them know that Heavenly Father will be there for them too.

The wonderful little book, *Heaven is For Real* by Marc Burpo, is a true story which gives the account of his little four year old boy who is given the privilege of seeing Heaven for himself. In it, he declares the veracity of a Celestial realm, and I recommend it to believers and non-believers alike. I love that book, and to it I add my testimony that there is indeed, a very loving Heavenly Father waiting for us there, with His Son Jesus Christ and the Holy Ghost. Together, the three of them preside in the Heavens. They are real, and love and care for us beyond measure.

That being said, the opposite is also true: the adversary is real as well.

The scriptures tell us that "...the devil, as a roaring lion, walketh about, seeking whom he may devour" (1 Peter 5:8). There are many devices he uses, and cunning ways with which he would love to take us down. Through his clever snares, social mores have dropped drastically in my lifetime. Regrettably, it's not just men that Satan has fooled in recent times. What was once easily discernible as black and white, right or wrong, has sadly morphed into *fifty shades of grey*.

Just another moment on Lucifer for some personal commentary, then I won't waste any more time on him. He is, and was a megalomaniac from the beginning.

Somebody has to have the guts to say it.

To envision someone wanting to take glory and praise from our Beautiful Heavenly Father — it is just unfathomable. Gratefully, the numbers of those who follow him to the fullest will be few in this life. Fortunate are we if we only come across one or two of them in our own earthly sojourn. These minions of his would be so benighted and dark in their ways that their own misery would not be enough. They, too, would desire to drag us down, in an attempt to control our eternal destiny as well.

Remember:

When you try to control everything, you enjoy nothing. Relax. Breathe. Let it go.

We should use all caution to keep from his ways. If the devil is knocking at the door, don't answer. After all, no one wants to be like Satan, the Ultimate Control-Freak.

As the scriptures say, the Devil is as dangerous as a wild beast, and he laughs at what he's been able to accomplish. We would be wise to never let our guard down, as he does have certain powers while he wanders the earth. It was revealed to the Prophet Joseph Smith that in the last days "no flesh shall be safe upon the waters"and that"the destroyer rideth upon the face thereof"(D&C 61:14-19).

Without the intervention of He who created the vast waters of earth, perhaps the adversary has indeed brought about the end of many men thru the ages while on the open seas. We know those waters are made still that hear the Savior's gentle command, or made powerful like the parting of the Red Sea. They are obedient to Him, their Creator.

That was my experience, and I will forever boast of His everlasting strength and mighty power and grace. What else can compare? I've seen it up close and personal, and don't expect to see another manifestation like it ever again. I've also learned to be more sensitive to the quiet whisperings of the Spirit, as I know it rarely if ever, comes audibly as it did that day at the beach.

Since then, I've come to appreciate His awesome creative power thru the beautiful design that I see in the night skies above. The Heavens are perfectly organized and God has stated that they should be considered as "signs and wonders" (Genesis 1:14). There they are, for all of us to see — the 'signs' that the sign seekers are looking for.

I started to go on pre-dawn walks for exercise, and began looking up at the incredible stars and constellations. I earned the astronomy merit badge as a thirteen year old boy scout while out on Catalina Island, but now, with a little life experience behind me, I have a deeper appreciation for it all. It's so quiet at that hour with no traffic, I'm able to focus on the beauty above me, and take in the expanse like never before. While I do so, I pray to Heavenly Father for help and guidance in the coming day's work. I thank Him for the magnificent view, and I also always remember to thank Him for His Kindness for the second chance at life that He gave me.

Back at home, we have a four-foot "GIVE THANKS" sign hanging in the dining room of our little farmhouse. It's not only for mealtime, but it also helps us remember, first and foremost — to have an attitude of gratitude for life and all that we have together.

Each year in late August when my boys were little, I'd be on one side of a birthday cake blazing with candles, and through the flames I'd see their smiling faces looking back at me. They'd wait for me to blow out the big fire, and every year I silently made my one wish: the hope that my three sons would always be thankful. Then I'd tell them what I wished for, with a little reminder from the scriptures that says, "And in nothing doth man offend God, or against none is his wrath kindled, save those who confess not his hand in all things…" (D&C 59:21). Always remember Him!

I didn't want to sound preachy, but it was God's hand that preserved me, and therefore, He also preserved our family and our lives together.

Without the second part of the miracle — when the

messenger came, and I finally learned the truth — the whole experience would have just remained an interesting story and not the miracle it was.

I am not ashamed of the Gospel of Jesus Christ, nor am I of the incredible tender mercies that He has extended to me. As the saying goes: where much — no, let me say it this way — WHERE MUCH HAS BEEN GIVEN — I feel much is required of me, and I expect to spend the rest of my days praising Heavenly Father for his goodness.

I've told my boys that if we will keep our minds from being poisoned by the evils that Satan tries to make cool and popular — God will do great things for us (Alma 26:22). He will bless us for our efforts if we seek Him. As Latter-day Saints, we believe He will reveal many great and important things which pertain to His kingdom, and He does so.

We believe in personal revelation. It may not be a miracle on the ocean, but we all experience His presence in our lives. Great or small, miracles do happen.

Take the miracle of healing for example. Think of the excruciating pain that we feel with a small paper cut or hang-nail. The Bible teaches that we are "fearfully and wonderfully made" (Psalms 139:14). Some translations say "beautifully and wonderfully made." Both are true. Through His divine creation, our bodies miraculously heal themselves. The shooting pain of a split finger that consumed our thoughts subsides after only a few days. These are small miracles He provides for us.

Through the Atonement of His Son, Jesus Christ, all of life's sorrows and suffering will one day end. While small pains may take only a few days, life's deeper cuts require more time to heal. One day all of our tears will be wiped away.

The greatest event of all time enables each of us to experience that which President Kimball called the *Miracle of Forgiveness*. Thru the Atonement of Jesus Christ, we can be partakers of this miracle of all miracles. He will be our Savior, and we can say that His word has become "a lamp unto my feet, and a light unto my path" as stated in Psalms 119:105. It's a blessing, and something of a miracle — knowing that He is present in our lives in spite of problems and challenges.

As we navigate thru life's rough waters, we would do well to listen to our mothers and our loving wives, who often are the ones who see the danger and call out to us in warning. Recognize that God's very Priesthood Power is on the earth today, and learn to cherish His council that He imparts thru His chosen servants, line upon line.

I began this little book by telling about my friend, Angel Avila Ochoa. He sought liberty, and God helped him make it to freedom's shore. Here, he flourished at whatever job he did to earn a living. He loved life, and he blessed many people, including me. He was 64 years young when he passed away and went on to his eternal reward.

His brief obituary read that he is "free at last."

It was such a nice little funeral. It reminded me of an old Kenny Rogers song, called *Reuben James*. It's an up-tempo country song praising the life of a sharecropper, his kindness, and ultimately, his passing. In it, Kenny laments while singing *"…to your lonely pine box came — just a preacher, me and the rain. Just to sing one last refrain for Reuben James."*

And then he adds:

"Reuben James, well you still walk the Pearly Fields of my mind …I loved you then and I love you now, Reuben James."

And so it was — and is, with my friend Angel.

Besides the funeral director and an aide from the nursing home, three others planned to attend with me. Knowing this, I invited the elders to join us, thinking that they could sing a hymn and make the service a little nicer. The mission office sent six elders and two sisters. Together, we joined them for a beautiful Spanish rendition of *"God Be with*

You 'Till We Meet Again." Afterwards, on my drive home, I thought that I wouldn't mind it one bit if my own memorial service one day was small and sweet — kind of like Angel's.

His life will always be a blessed memory for me, and he does still"walk the pearly fields of my mind." He lived according to the principles spoken of so eloquently by Dr. Martin Luther King on August 28, 1963. In the speech which won him the Nobel Peace Prize the following year, he dreamed that his four little children would"one day live in a nation where they will not be judged by the color of their skin, but by the content of their character."

Angel lived his life like all men were his brothers, and he was right.

In the Washington D.C. Temple there is a large 30-foot mural depicting the second coming of Jesus Christ. The Lord, with outstretched hands, is standing before numerous people from all nationalities and races. Many are kneeling before the Prince of Peace in adoring worship, while others are not. We will want to be among those on His right hand at the last day, and not on His left, as depicted.

In my view, this painting depicts the fulfillment of Reverend King's dream. That will be a glorious gathering, and we all have a part to play in bringing it to fruition.

Do your part. Hasten the work. Fulfill the dream.

In the *Book of Mormon*, the prophet Alma wished for the voice of an angel, so that he might speak with power. Through this little book, I've had the privilege of being Angel's voice. His story is powerful, and his life was remarkable. I hope that one day I'll be able to find his daughter, so I can tell her of his great influence in my life. Perhaps one day missionaries will even go to Cuba from the other islands of the Caribbean.

If there is one lesson from my entire experience that I would like to share with my family and others, it would be —

that God is not only there, He is very much aware — of you, your circumstances, and of your every need. I'm not certain if it is through our guardian angels, or His personal Omni-science — but I know that He does know.

If you ever feel insignificant, small and unimportant, or think that God is simply too busy with other pressing matters to be concerned about you, please reconsider. Remember, when someone is nasty or treats you poorly, don't take it personally. It says nothing about you, but a lot about them.

Heaven is watching over all, and will send Divine Assis-tance to us on earth, even if we are considered to be among the least of these our brethren.

Miracles haven't ceased. God's angels do minister to His children on the earth. I know this because they've minis-tered to me. I know that one day I'll see Angel again, when we meet on that beautiful distant shore. I'll also find out who the four young men were in the water with me that day. I don't think I'll have to search far and wide though, as I believe their names were Christopher, Michael, Andrew and Gabriel. For you see, I do believe they were my own sons.

This was taken on my mail route in Kaysville, where we work, live, and worship.

Angel Ochoa

Angel Ochoa passed away Aug. 31, 2013 in Ogden, UT. Born Feb. 21, 1949 in Cuba. "Fleeing Castro's Grasp - 20 years hence- "Con mí família, I'm free at last, free at last!"

Matthew 23:12

*Thanks to family and friends who helped in
getting this ready for publication.*

*Extra kudos to my lifelong friend and mentor Lee Murphy,
from California, who's been bugging me for over ten years to put
pen to paper. Well, here it is, so stop harassing me. Just kidding!
No, I'm not.*

*Special thanks goes to two people who I consider
collaborators on the project:*

*First and foremost — my dear mother. Mom, I'll always cherish
the sweet memory of many nights with you sitting at the computer
with me. Thank you again for your incredible patience and
unfailing encouragement. Your skills got it off the ground floor.
Without your help, this book probably would have forever
remained a nice story in pen and ink in a spiral binder
at my house. I simply couldn't have done it without you.*

*My friend Pat Hill, who I've known since we were teenagers at
Bountiful High, has been the other indispensable part of this little
project. Your artistic talent has made this work a viable product,
and I'll always be grateful for your good-natured humor.
Your years of work in layout and design were invaluable,
and took it to the next level. Nice job, Lancelot!*

*To my wife Tauna — Eternal thanks.
Without you, there would be no me.*

*And to my boys — well, let's just say, I hope I can someday
return the favor, and come to your rescue.*